Poem and Symbol
A Brief History of French Symbolism

OTHER BOOKS BY WALLACE FOWLIE

Rimbaud: A Critical Study
Mallarmé
A Reading of Proust
A Reading of Dante's Inferno
André Gide: His Life and Art
Paul Claudel
Stendhal
The French Critic
Climate of Violence: The French Literary Tradition from Baudelaire to
    the Present
Dionysus in Paris: A Guide to Contemporary French Theatre
Age of Surrealism
The Clown's Grail: A Study of Love in Its Literary Expression
French Literature: Its History and Its Meaning
Characters from Proust: Poems
Letters of Henry Miller and Wallace Fowlie
Journal of Rehearsals: A Memoir
Aubade: A Teacher's Notebook
Sites: A Third Memoir

TRANSLATIONS

Complete Works of Rimbaud
Two Dramas by Claudel
A Poet Before the Cross by Claudel
Seamarks by Saint-John Perse
Don Juan by Molière
The Miser by Molière
Classical French Drama (five plays)
Mid-Century French Poets
Sixty Poems of Scève

Poem & Symbol

A
Brief History
of
French Symbolism

Wallace Fowlie

The Pennsylvania State University Press
University Park and London

Library of Congress Cataloging-in-Publication Data

Fowlie, Wallace, 1908–
    Poem and symbol : a brief history of French symbolism / Wallace
Fowlie.
        p.   cm.
    Includes bibliographical references.
    ISBN 0-271-00683-8
    ISBN 0-271-00696-X (pbk.)
    1. French literature—19th century—History and criticism.
2. French literature—20th century—History and criticism.
3. Symbolism.   I. Title.
PQ295.S9F69   1990
841.009′15—dc20   89–16120

The paper used in this publication meets the minimum requirements of
American National Standard for Information Sciences—Permanence of
Paper for Printed Library Materials, ANSI Z39.48–1984.

To John Dunaway

Contents

1

The Background of Symbolism: From Romanticism to Art for Art's Sake

Romanticism has always been looked upon as a literary revolution. It was the first in the history of French literature that cannot be separated from a comparable revolution in painting. The *Salon* of 1827, the painting exhibit held the same year the *Préface de Cromwell* was read and published by Victor Hugo, showed Delacroix's *Le Christ au jardin des Oliviers* and the work of a twenty-one-year-old artist, Louis Boulanger, a painting called *Mazeppa*, which was enthusiastically received by the painters. Boulanger became momentarily Hugo's favorite painter.

This union of poetry and art was further consecrated by another *cénacle*, quite different from Hugo's, which is sometimes considered the birthplace of the movement called *l'art pour l'art*. It was a studio workshop, an *atelier*, on the rue du Doyenné, today replaced by the Place du Carrousel, in front of the Louvre. The two leaders and spokesmen of the group were Théophile Gautier and Gérard de Nerval.

The word *rapin*, first designating a fine-arts student, and then, by extension, a "bohemian" artist, is most apt in describing the type of artist frequenting the meetings of friends in the rue du Doyenné. The *rapins* were eccentrics, hostile to all bourgeois standards, truculent in their behavior, often very gifted, and usually representing failures in their vocation.

At the beginning of his career, Théophile Gautier hesitated between painting and poetry. When he finally chose poetry, he brought to it the style, ideas, and habits of the painting studio. In his book *Les Jeunes-France*, he gave an animated picture of the young "left-wing" romantics.

The questions relating to "art for art's sake" have been raised in every age, but the phrase in its most precise meaning applies to this French movement, originating with Gautier, Nerval, and Pétrus Borel, in their avowed aversion to the bourgeois spirit and Saint-Simonianism, or humanitarianism. Most scholars agree that the first reference to *l'art pour l'art* is in a work by the philosopher Victor Cousin, *Questions esthétiques et religieuses* (1818), in which he says that art is not enrolled in the service of religion and morals or in the service of what is pleasing and useful. Art exists for its own self: *"Il faut de la religion pour la religion, de la morale pour la morale, et de l'art pour l'art."*

With the founding of the Second Empire, in 1852, the opposition between those writers concerned with the defense of a national morality and the cause of progress and those representing the tradition of art for art's sake became clear. In his preface to the *Poèmes antiques* (1852), Leconte de Lisle quarrels with everyone on every subject, and sees the political future sullied for a long time with bourgeois meanness, industrialism, and utilitarianism. As the politics of the Second Empire (1852–70) continued, the younger writers and artists looked for a new faith not in participation in active life but in rejuvenated forms of art.

The "bourgeois" art of the day had no originality and no style, according to the strong attacks made against it by Baudelaire, Flaubert, Gautier, Leconte de Lisle, and Théodore de Banville. The younger Hugo of 1830 was still revered, and Alfred de Vigny was respected for having said that a book must be composed, cut and sculptured as if it were a statue of Parian marble. Gautier represented the continuation of that tradition. Baudelaire regretted having come too late, after the glorious days of romanticism, after *le coucher de soleil romantique*. At the end of his career Gautier, in his *Histoire du romantisme*, spoke of the early period as a golden age.

The beginnings of the new movement, between 1851 and 1853, resembled the beginnings of romanticism. The new bohemianism was celebrated and idealized. Henri Murger is perhaps the best historian of this renaissance, in *Scènes de la vie de Bohème* (1851), a novel made famous years later by Puccini in his opera *La Bohème*.

In reality, there was no "school" uniting such different temperaments as Flaubert and Renan, the Goncourts, and Leconte de Lisle. But there were common aspirations and a belief in the principle of the independence of art. The historian of Parnassian art, Catulle Mendès, went to great pains to point out that Le Parnasse never represented a school. It was a theory—a doctrine—similar to art for art's sake, a form of faith coming directly from romanticism. Théophile Gautier was the central figure. He had proclaimed as early as 1835 the doctrine of art for art's sake in the preface to his novel *Mlle de Maupin*.

Flaubert admired Gautier, and at least during the early part of his career considered himself Gautier's disciple. Both were joined in their dislike for their contemporary world. In his home in Neuilly, Gautier often received at his Thursday dinners Flaubert, Banville, Jules and Edmond Goncourt, and Baudelaire. Baudelaire, who had probably met Gautier for the first time in 1849 at the Hôtel Pimodan, where both of them lived briefly, dedicated *Les Fleurs du Mal* to Gautier:

> *Au poète impeccable, au parfait magicien ès lettres françaises, au très cher et au très vénéré maître et ami.*

> (To the impeccable poet, to the perfect magician of French Letters, to the very dear and very venerated master and friend.)

Gautier, in his turn, wrote the laudatory introduction to the complete works of Baudelaire.

The new poets were published in three anthologies by the publisher Lemerre in 1866, 1869, and 1877, under the title *Le Parnasse Contemporain*. The word *parnassien* can be applied to theories of *l'art pour l'art*. There was very little development or change in these theories after 1870. Gautier died in 1872. Flaubert seemed to look upon the new democracy, the Third Republic, as the end of art. He was convinced that a reign of utilitarianism was going to triumph: *"Nous allons devenir un grand pays plat et industriel comme la Belgique"*

("We are going to become a great flat industrial country like Belgium").

For about fifty years the principles of art for art's sake (Parnassianism) were current in France. Belief in the artist's freedom was clearly stated in Hugo's preface to *Cromwell*, but the specific doctrines themselves were analyzed and clarified best in Flaubert's letters and the Goncourts' journal, the prefaces of Leconte de Lisle, and the critical writing of Baudelaire.

Flaubert was the least charitable of these writers. He examined the French bourgeoisie as if it were a world reserved for his research, and collected a long series of extracts from conversations he had overheard, out of which he compiled the *Dictionnaire des idées reçues*. He and Baudelaire referred endlessly to examples of bourgeois stupidity—*la bêtise*, as they called it.

These French writers and artists often analyzed the difficulties in creating the kind of work that would match their ideals. Their pages on the slow, painful process of artistic creation are among their most valuable contributions. The achievement of anything like perfection requires time and labor and constant revision. The emotions of the artist in the process of creating his art are brilliantly studied in Delacroix's *Journal*, in Flaubert's correspondence, and in the Goncourts' journals. But whereas romanticism emphasized the sentiments and sorrows of the individual, the Parnassian creed emphasized the artist's passion for beauty, which separates a man from everything that is vulgar and banal.

The principal theories on morality and art, as developed by Flaubert, Baudelaire, and the Goncourts, are still the bases for the aesthetics of modern art. These writers would say that truth is not immoral, and art is not immoral. Obscurity is immoral only when it is untruthful. Intellectual honesty is a leading characteristic of the true artist, and such honesty is in itself a moral principle. Such men, for whom art is almost a religion (Flaubert, Baudelaire, Mallarmé, Joyce, Henry James, T. S. Eliot), were morally unified in their temperaments and in the scrupulousness with which they carried out their work as artists.

Art contains in itself its own principle of morality. With this thought in mind, the exponents of *l'art pour l'art* advanced the theory that there is more moral integrity in a work of art when it is devoid of a specific moralizing intention. A vigorous, bold depiction of vice and passion can have a moral effect on the public. The morality of a great artist is in the forcefulness and the truthfulness of his treatment of whatever subject he chooses. In other words, the morality is in the form of the art and not in its subject matter.

From *L'art pour l'art* to *Le symbolisme* and *La décadence*

When Sainte-Beuve used the phrase "ivory tower" to designate Alfred de Vigny's retreat from the world and from the activities of Paris, he could not have realized how the phrase would be used subsequently by those exponents of *l'art pour l'art* to describe precisely the site of the artist's isolation—not for the purpose of exile, not to manifest his scorn for the world of everyday actuality, but for the purpose of understanding his world more deeply and discovering the means of expressing his thought in a richer and more original manner. The ivory tower (*la tour d'ivoire*) was used this way, with this precise meaning, by Flaubert and Henry James, by Pound and James Joyce, by Proust in his cork-lined room, by Eliot, and by Yeats.

The word associated with Baudelaire in the new aesthetic credo was *bizarre*. In announcing in his *salon* of 1855 that "le beau est toujours bizarre" ("beauty is always strange"), he indicated that the artist's attraction to the strange is an element of his personality and separates him from most men, who submit easily to the conventional and the traditional, who prefer not to be startled by originality. Those impulses that often manifest themselves in the subconscious—fantasies, hallucinations, and sentiments of fear—and which in most men are not allowed to develop represent the sources of experiences in man's moral and physical life. The artist, for Baudelaire, feels a desire to know and explore such fantasies that border on dreams and nightmares.

The word *maudit* ("cursed"), used by Verlaine in three essays in 1883 to characterize the new type of poet, was more aggressive than the word *bizarre*. The three poets he discussed were Corbière, Rimbaud, and Mallarmé—"Satanic" poets whom normally constituted citizens would repulse through fear that their work contained the germs of dissolution.

More vigorously than the essays of Verlaine, J. K. Huysmans's novel *A rebours* (1884) developed the theme of decadence in art. The book's protagonist, Des Esseintes, represents Huysman's philosophical pessimism about the world, strongly reminiscent of Schopenhauer's thought, and a horror for what he considered the stupidity of most people and the malice of fate.

Des Esseintes is as refined as the comte de Montesquiou (who participated later in the makeup of Charlus in Proust's *A la recherche du temps perdu*). The tapestries in his house are chosen as carefully as the bindings of his books. The sensations of smell are as acute for him as they were for Baudelaire. Indeed all forms of sensuality are celebrated as if they were part of a mystical cult. Perfumes have an effect on his spiritual life. He creates symphonies of smells as if he were illustrating Baudelaire's sonnet *Correspondances* and the doctrine of synesthesia. He is as refined in his analysis of sensations as he is unusual in his taste for so-called decadent literature. In modern literature his predilections start with Baudelaire and continue with Poe, Ernest Hello, Jules Barbey d'Aurevilly, Verlaine, Corbière, Mallarmé. Neurosis and decadence (*névrose, décadence*) are terms freely expressed throughout the novel, in Des Esseintes's passion for the paintings of Gustave Moreau and Odilon Redon.

A rebours (Against the Grain) created a sensation. It revealed to a fairly wide public the work of the *poètes maudits* as continuing the work of the Parnassians and illustrating the renewed belief in *l'art pour l'art*. Such works and such theories formed the basis for attitudes that were struck in the 1890s in France and England, often referred to as aesthetic and decadent attitudes. The history of taste and morals and aesthetics is difficult to describe chronologically. The English terms "gay nineties" and "mauve decade" and the French term *fin de siècle* are applicable to at least fifty years of literary and art history.

In 1883, a poem of Verlaine, *Langueur*, called attention to the word *décadence*. The opening line is the poet's self-portrait as he calls himself "the 'empire' at the end of the age of decadence": "*Je suis l'Empire à la fin de la décadence.*" In England, where the term was associated with certain aspects of French civilization, writers were, on the whole, worried about the term being attached to them. To offset the evil implied in the word "decadence" and a purely aesthetic view of life, comic elements were added. The tone of dead seriousness in *A rebours* is quite altered in Oscar Wilde's *Picture of Dorian Gray*. English levity offset French grimness. Swinburne, as well as Wilde, was able to parody himself. The high camp of Wilde and Max Beerbohm probably testifies to an English reticence and puritanism in the face of French extravagance and "immorality."

The thesis that Wilde develops so brilliantly in his essay "The Critic as Artist" (in his book *Intentions*) is one of the significant contributions to be drawn from the entire movement of *l'art pour l'art*.

Undoubtedly inspired by Gustave Moreau's paintings, Wilde's play *Salomé* (written in French), in which the heroine is turned into a sadist, was one of the more serious English contributions. But even here, the seriousness of the text was parodied by Aubrey Beardsley's illustrations. Arthur Symons, in his analysis of what he called "the decadent movement in literature," did not minimize the French sources and examples. He called decadence a "beautiful disease" and suggested that a more appropriate name to use was "symbolism." This may have influenced Symons in naming his book-length study of 1899 *The Symbolist Movement in Literature*. The words "decadent" and "aesthetic" were thereby given in England a healthier terminology. Corruption was given a new chance and a new garb.

At the time, during the Second Empire, when art for art's sake came into its own, Gautier, perhaps because of his limitations, or perhaps because he never felt with the intensity of a Baudelaire, reached a degree of impassiveness in his behavior and outlook and gave in his writing the clearest example of a belief in laborious, difficult technique. In his poem *L'Art*, printed in the second edition of *Emaux et Camées*, in 1857, he defined the precept that only those forms of art that are technically difficult and demanding of an artist's patience have any chance for survival. The harder the material is to work in, the more beautiful the work will be. Gautier lists as examples: first, poetry, and then marble, onyx, and enamel:

> *Oui, l'oeuvre sort plus belle*
> *D'une forme au travail*
>   *Rebelle*
> *Vers, marbre, onyx, émail.*

> (Yes, the work emerges more beautiful
> from a form
> rebellious to labor
> Poetry, marble, onyx, enamel.)

If these requirements of robustness and strength are met, the piece of sculpture and the poem, whose versification is complex, will endure longer than the city.

Tout passe.—L'art robuste
Seul a l'éternité:
Le buste
Survit à la cité.

(Everything disappears—Robust art
alone is eternal:
The Bust survives the city.)

Ezra Pound, in *Mauberley* (1920), recapitulated this theory of Gautier
and imitated the versification of the French poem. The art of Flaubert is compared to Penelope's tapestry, patiently and everlastingly
begun over again each day in the artist's hope to reach perfection:

His true Penelope

Was Flaubert
And his tool
The engraver's

Firmness
Not the full smile
His art, but an art
In profile.

In an earlier poem, *L'Hippopotame*, Gautier described the new
attitude of the Parnassian poet by comparing his indifference to the
hostile world of the bourgeoisie and the traditional critics with
the thick hide of the hippopotamus. The poet's convictions, his
aloofness and aloneness, were evoked in the hippo's stolid heavi-
ness as he wanders through the jungles of Java:

L'hippopotame au large ventre
Habite aux jungles de Java . . .
Je suis comme l'hippopotame:
De ma conviction couvert.

(The hippopotamus with the huge belly
Inhabits the jungles of Java . . .
I am like the hippopotamus:
    Protected by my conviction.)

Eliot wrote the same kind of poem, in terms of form and tone, in
The Hippopotamus, but gave a different meaning to the metaphor by
comparing the hippopotamus to the Church of Rome:

The 'potamus can never reach
The mango on the mango-tree;
But fruits of pomegranate and peach
Refresh the Church from over sea.

The cult of formal beauty and the application of elaborate technique were always present in art for art's sake. And in France, the
passion behind this cult was, to some extent, hatred of successful
mediocrity. The ascetic dignity and conscientiousness that Leconte
de Lisle in *Poèmes antiques* and Heredia in his *Trophées* gave to pure
craftsmanship were admired by the English—by Swinburne, for
example—but the art was never directly copied by them. The French
prose writers had perhaps more tangible influence. Walter Pater's
essay "Style" recapitulates theories of Flaubert.

It is impossible to estimate how much Baudelaire's so-called mor-
bidity and taste for extracting beauty from unusual experiences
developed because of his hatred for the world in which he lived.
At one time, and not very long ago, Baudelaire was looked upon,
both in England and France, as an isolated psychopathic case.
Today, largely because of Eliot's three essays on him, he is studied
in England and America as the modern poet—the modern Dante,
in fact—who has given to the doctrine of morality in art its
profoundest meaning. The wide range of themes in contemporary
poetry, extending from the classical theme of Gregory Corso's poem
Uccello to the lyrics of Bob Dylan and Jim Morrison, is owed in some
degree to Baudelaire's example.

The word "symbolism" has come to have as many meanings as
"romanticism." Ibsen's plays and Wagner's operas have been called
"symbolist." For some, decadence became a means to religious
conversion—in the cases, for example, of Barbey d'Aurevilly and
Verlaine. Rimbaud's *Une Saison en Enfer* and *Les Illuminations* played

a part in Paul Claudel's return to his faith. The decadent symbolist Huysmans of *A rebours* became a Catholic in *Là-Bas* (1891).

At the very end of the century, several events seemed to make clear that art for art's sake and its survival in decadence were over. The triumph of Edmond Rostand's play *Cyrano de Bergerac* in 1897 indicated that the public wanted heroes and sentiment, action and wit. The Dreyfus affair encouraged many writers to turn into fighters. Nationalism, an outgrowth of imperialism, was pioneered by Maurice Barrès, whose cult of human energy was an attack on art for art's sake. In England, Rudyard Kipling put his art in the service of energy and imperialism. The odor of decadence diminished before the socialism of Jean Jaurès and Zola and Anatole France. Yet some disciples of art for art's sake did survive. The turn-of-the-century movements did continue their work far into the century, although never occupying a central position in their day: Pierre Louÿs in France, for example, and George Moore in England.

The 1920s were characterized by the appearance of many forms of art for art's sake: a philosophical pessimism, an archsophistication, a renewed interest in literary techniques, the emergence of somewhat defiant forms of immorality. Abbé Bremond's discussion with Paul Valéry over the theory of *poésie pure* was a worthy topic for art for art's sake. In describing European art in 1925, José Ortega y Gasset called it "new," and yet the traits he analyzed are those we associate with the pure art created in an ivory tower.

Such a doctrine as *l'art pour l'art* can be born and develop only in a blatantly materialistic age. The prosperity of Louis Napoleon's era, when Gautier, Baudelaire, and Flaubert wrote their best works, was not unlike the Victorian atmosphere of austerity in which Oscar Wilde and Walter Pater flourished. The letters exchanged between Gide and Valéry from 1890 to 1910 refer frequently to the uselessness of art and the characteristic of art as not serving any definable function. The type of man unable to understand and feel art is Flaubert's pharmacist, Homais, in *Madame Bovary*. He was the type easy to scandalize. *"Epater le bourgeois"* (scandalize the bourgeois) had once served almost as a battle cry. In America he was to become Sinclair Lewis's Babbitt. Such literary creations as Homais and Babbitt inevitably beget art for art's sake.

Since the time Jean-Jacques Rousseau revealed so much of himself in his *Confessions* to a public eager to know the personal details of his life, the artist's life and personality have been a part of literary study. There have been two moments in the history of literary criticism when marked opposition to biography was felt: in the

1930s in America, in the "new criticism," the back-to-the text movement, and in the 1950s and 1960s in France, with the structuralist critics. From Rousseau's day on, despite the fact that most artists have led quite conventional lives, the general public has grown to believe that they are temperamental and irresponsible, if not immoral.

The great importance given to aesthetic theories in Baudelaire's generation, theories either identical with those of art for art's sake or closely related to them, tended to conceal or disguise the moral and philosophical problems felt by that generation. An attitude toward life that in the age of romanticism was called *le mal du siècle* is in evidence at the end of the century, when it is called *le mal de fin de siècle*. Paul Bourget's *Essais* and *Nouveaux Essais de Psychologie Contemporaine* (1883 and 1885) still offer today a penetrating analysis of a drama taking place in the moral conscience of a generation. The suffering studied by Bourget was more than the familiar phase of melancholy that most young people go through when their world seems limited and their aspirations limitless. It was something more than introversion. The poetry of Jules Laforgue reveals many aspects of a dissatisfaction and even resentment that had to do with the prodigious development of the large cities, with the monotony of provincial life, with the routine existence of employees and civil servants (*fonctionnaires*), and with *la vie quotidienne* in general, coming after two generations of romanticism in the arts in which individualism had been exalted.

Baudelaire occupied a central position in the Bourget essays as the artist who had the courage to call himself a decadent and adopt an attitude of sympathy with artificiality and strangeness. The mysterious word *décadence* would seem to mean the will of the artist to understand the basic drives of his nature, to explain what Baudelaire called the "inner abyss" or "cemetery" of the self, and to use the creation of art as a remedy for "ennui" or "spleen," or what might be called by the simpler term "pessimism."

The artists in France in 1885 were far more cut off psychologically and sociologically from society than their elders had been in 1820. Their suffering was more neurotic and morbid. Their inability to adapt to society was more radical. The themes of their poetry were more personal, more introverted, more symptomatic of serious psychological upheavals. A fatigue with life is at the basis of such a poem as Baudelaire's *Chant d'automne*. A disenchantment with everything that life had promised him pervades the verse of Jules Laforgue. The need to escape from the mortal boredom of provincial life is studied in Flaubert as well as in the poetry of the decadents. The desperate need to live in a distant legendary land is sung by Verlaine in *Les Fêtes Galantes*, by Baudelaire in *L'Invitation au voyage*, and by almost all of the lesser poets during the last part of the century. But finally, dreams themselves become impossible and all hope disappears. Albert Samain, in *Au jardin de l'infante*, says that the sense of the void, of nothingness, has forged a new soul for him: *"Et le néant m'a fait une âme comme lui."*

Around 1890, the proliferation in Paris of literary magazines was proof that *le symbolisme* had grown into something comparable to a movement. *La Vogue, La Plume, L'Ermitage,* and *Le Mercure de France* provided the new writers with the means of publishing and propagating those trends of the new literature that still preserved from the earlier Parnassian days an emphasis on art forms, especially those forms that would bring out the musical qualities of language. Less importance was granted to the shape and color of objects, those plastic qualities celebrated by the Parnassians. There were new traces of moral and psychological preoccupations, of metaphysical problems, and of a style of writing more impressionistic than Parnassian.

At the Saturday night gatherings in the Latin Quarter, under the auspices of *La Plume*, the Bohemian extravaganzas and enthusiasms for art recalled the rue du Doyenné meetings, where Gautier and Nerval once discussed their theories. Yet, on the whole, the *fin de siècle* gatherings were less bohemian than those of the *rapins* of 1835. Pierre Louÿs warned his new friends André Gide and Paul Valéry that Heredia was a *mondain* and that Mallarmé was so serious and correct in his behavior that they would have to give up wearing their wide-brimmed hats and long neckties. Mallarmé's *mardis* had almost an official air about them in 1890. At least in a social sense, Mallarmé had won out over Verlaine. The *salon* had replaced the *café*.

While Gide was still attending the "Tuesdays" of Mallarmé, he wrote and published a manifesto on art that, although it was subtitled *théorie du symbole*, was also a recapitulation of Parnassian theories on the role of the artist and his quest. The full title was *Traité du Narcisse*. Narcissus is the man seeking to find his own image and who sees at the same time the image of everything else in the world. Narcissus is presented by Gide as the myth of man's return to the beginning of time, when all forms were paradisaical and crystalline. Poetry is the nostalgia for Paradise that has been lost. Adam had seen this wonder before he had seen himself. When, according to

Gide's interpretation of the myth, he saw himself, he then distinguished himself from everything else, and fell from grace.

By defining the poet as the man able to look, able to see Paradise behind appearance, Gide indicated affiliations with one part of the Parnassian creed. Every phenomenon is the symbol of a truth. The poet's duty is to manifest it. As the poet contemplates the symbols of the world, he penetrates at the same time their deepest meanings. This is why Gide calls the work of art a crystal, a partial paradise where the idea unfolds as a flower does, in its original purity. As an admirer of Mallarmé, Gide, in *Traité du Narcisse*, wrote a profession of faith in platonic idealism.

The symbol of Mallarmé's art, which can be as visible and precise as in Parnassian art—a swan, a vase, a faun—is the poet's creation, capable of suggesting. *Suggérer* is a key word in Mallarmé's aesthetics. It means first to awaken, to indicate without specifically naming or defining, to propose a meaning without dogmatically imposing it. *Suggérer* can also mean to incite and prolong an emotion on the part of the reader. During the decade of the 1890s, Mallarmé and his disciples enlarged the meaning of the symbol to include certain aspects of myth and allegory. Whereas an allegory is primarily didactic, a myth is addressed as much to the emotions of the reader as to his intelligence. It tends more to move him than to convince him. Allegory is therefore moralistic and myth is religious by nature. The object in Parnassian art and the symbol in symbolist art are primarily aesthetic, intended to give to the reader a sense of the beautiful. But the literary symbol, as it has been used since Baudelaire's time, in its aesthetic power, has a closer relationship with the religious spirit of man than with any reasonable, practical, or didactic use.

Symbolism has been a major study of literature since Baudelaire's *Correspondances*, which can be seen as a succinct manifesto. It has provided an aesthetic basis for works that have elements of both myth and allegory. They are among the most impressive literary works since 1850, which have reacted strongly against a realistic art of precision in order to reflect preoccupations that are religious and philosophical: the poetry of Rimbaud and Mallarmé, Yeats and Eliot; the novels of Proust and Joyce.

It would be difficult to exaggerate the prevalence of pessimism throughout Europe between 1880 and 1900—the doubts and reservations expressed about science, the influence of Schopenhauer's philosophy, the negativism of Ibsen and Nietzsche. The aesthetic beliefs, often designated as "decadent," came in part from the spread of intellectual and moral pessimism, from an exalting of Baudelaire's thesis concerning the decadence of aging civilizations.

From today's perspective, it is fairly clear that decadence was one aspect of the development of symbolism. Stefan George's activities were efforts without any subversive characteristics, intended to rally young German writers around a set of beliefs that were almost identical with art for art's sake. English decadence was more complex to follow and understand, and in fact was so complex that the word "decadence" seemed inappropriate. It was used, however, because of the scorn on the part of some writers for conventional morality and for certain morbid elements of art that were esteemed. The English origins for this cult for beauty may be found in the poetry of Keats in the early part of the century and later redefined and reformulated by Rossetti, Morris, and Swinburne. John Ruskin's teachings on aesthetics had a more direct influence, whereas the writings of Walter Pater rallied very little support. French influence was felt to some extent in the work of Swinburne and Pater, but especially in the writings of George Moore. In the 1890s, when the figure of Oscar Wilde dominated all others, the movement of decadence was openly a revolt against tradition.

The cult of art for art's sake continued well into the twentieth century. The assumption of this cult, as illustrated by Joyce and Proust, would claim that art by itself is capable of conferring value and meaning upon life, and even ultimate value. Such writers as Yeats, Eliot, and Pound, who were in closest sympathy with the theories of art for art's sake and whose work reflects strong influences of those French writers associated with the movement, continued to show a similar attitude toward the world, at least toward the world of politics. They tended to look upon democracy as a standardizing process. Yeats felt almost a resentment for the prestige of science. They often gave evidence of a preference for an earlier social order. The cultural atmosphere of the early twentieth century was characterized by yearnings for the religious, the mystical, the occult, by the development of a new romanticism that merged with a belief in the sovereignty of the word in literature.

2

Gérard de Nerval:
The Disinherited

érard Labrunie, who later adopted the pseudonym Gérard
de Nerval, was born in 1808 and spent his first years in Le
Valois, the region north of Paris, where as a child he was
enchanted by the legends of the Ile-de-France. Later, in Paris, he
was a schoolmate and friend of Théophile Gautier, frequented the
cénacle on the rue du Doyenné, and played the role of dandy. He
became imbued with Germanic culture and translated in 1828 the
first part of Goethe's *Faust*.

For Nerval, the dream world was the world of the subconscious
controlled by its own laws. His works, and especially the sonnets
Les Chimères, are more than a distillation of experiences. They create
a new, compact life in which the settings are more real than the
landscapes of Le Valois, and the characters are more alive than
Adrienne, who kissed the poet's forehead in the children's *ronde* in
the park of the château when he was a boy, and more real than
Jenny Colon, the actress and singer in Paris with whom he fell in
love in 1836.

Nerval's wisdom was obscure because it was composed of mag-
netism, esotericism, and occultism, but his madness (he had two
serious mental crises, in 1841 and 1853) was lucid because it constructed his world of dreams. As a traveler, Nerval pursued the

symbolism of numbers and the memories of cabala, but as a poet he constructed the existence of a man who loves and suffers.

The figures of the women who inhabit his work resemble phantoms from a dream, Adrienne, Jenny Colon, a Neapolitan girl (*la brodeuse*), the English girl Octavie, are all synthesized into Aurélia, the only woman Gérard could love since, never having seen her in life, he was able to make her divine. Nerval encouraged his madness because it abolished time and plunged him into a distant past where all was illuminated with joy.

The conscious life of the poet was composed of departures, of voyages, of peregrinations, and only in his dreams did he remain immobilized before the ideal form of the woman he was seeking. A poet of love, Nerval always remained a poet of metempsychosis: he was never sure of loving, he was never sure of having loved, and only in his dreams was his former existence of Edenic purity, of innocence, and of happiness reproduced.

The children's dance during which he received a kiss from yellow-haired Adrienne marked the beginning of an experience of metempsychosis in which he believed he was all the youthful dancers of former times and in which so ancient a ceremonial kiss symbolized perfect happiness. The moment of ecstasy in our childhood, which in Gérard de Nerval's case was Adrienne's kiss, is the supreme moment in our amorous experience that we try during the rest of our life to recognize, to recapture, to relive in other forms with other beings.

The spiritual experience alone of love is tenacious. It inevitably triumphs over physical experience in binding us to time gone by, to a past that becomes present and future. Love is metempsychosis. It is the same experience we relive ceaselessly:

> *La treizième revient . . . C'est encor la première*

> (The thirteenth returns . . . it is still the first)

The sumptuous resonances of this sonnet of *Artémis* reduce the fragments of real experience into a single experience as simple as it is profound, as permanent as it is inaccessible.

Artémis is a luminous example of lyric creation in which the entire life of the poet is recast: all the idealism and all the failures. The sonnet not only contains direct reminiscences of nocturnal life, of death, of youth, and of maturity—it reproduces at the same time, through the miracle of coincidence and evocation, a universal expression of all men. *Artémis* diminishes life, in re-creating it, by use of the simplest words in all languages:

treize et *premier*	(*13* and *first*)
reine et *roi*	(*queen* and *king*)
berceau et *bière*	(*cradle* and *bier*)
aimer et *mourir*	(*to love* and *to die*)
rose et *sainte*	(*rose* and *saint*)

Paradoxically speaking, Nerval succeeds in doing in his sonnet what James Joyce does in *Finnegans Wake*, in the numerous closely covered pages of a long work: the re-creation of a life and of life. In each group of these primitive words of the sonnet, there exist worlds of involuntary memory. The subject matter of *Finnegans Wake* is these worlds, silenced in Nerval's sonnet, but obscurely living in the imagination of each reader. A work of art, truly, is not constructed on a subject matter; it is infallibly constructed on an absence. The void left by a completed experience is the authentic subject matter of art, and in a literary work, words come to fill this void without, however, building a real substance. An experience becomes spiritual from the moment it is translated into language. Art consecrates the spirituality of life by giving it a form, as the body consecrates the spirituality of the soul.

The principle of metempsychosis (revealed in the first line of *Artémis*), in the meaning of the words *treizième* and *première*), abolishes, by surpassing it, the tragic notion of love:

> *Et c'est toujours la seule—ou c'est le seul moment.*

(And it is still the only one—or it's the only moment.)

"The one moment" referred to was the love always sought by Nerval because it had once existed and because it continued to exist in his dreams. This dream is as imperishable as life itself, bequeathed to all men according to the mysterious principle of the survival of souls and things. Tragedy is therefore only the arresting of life and the death of dreams. Nerval never entered tragedy because his dream was an uninterrupted communication with the past, the survival of experience, the reality he asked of every day and every night. Nerval's poetry first abolished tragedy because of the fact that experience is never terminated, and then it abolished time, blotted out by the very character itself of dreams.

The purity of Nerval's imagination prevented him from becoming tragic. He was the victim without an executioner, extended on the altar, living, behind his closed eyes, the drama of life and death. Lying on his altar, where all possible voyages haunted him, he could see in his mind's eye the subtle skies of the Valois, the foggy forests of Ermenonville, the fields of Mortefontaine and Loisy. Gérard tried to identify himself with all the characters in life and in death, and to feel the destiny of each one in order to fill the abyss extending around him in all directions.

In one of his sonnets, *Le Christ aux Oliviers*, he said:

> . . . *si je meurs, c'est que tout va mourir!*

(If I die, everything is going to die!)

Therein he stated one of his most purely nihilistic philosophical thoughts. In this line he expresses his identity with the cosmos. In him cohabit the natural and the supernatural, and after him all will cease existing. The dreamer is a victim, and the worlds of his dream gravitate around the void. Nerval's work was an appeal, not for the purpose of justifying before his friends and physicians the attacks of madness that constantly threatened him, but for justifying his thoughts on the abyss and on renascent love.

As the perpetual vagrancy of his life led to suicide, his limitless dream coincided with the death of the world, with the extinction of the dark sun of melancholy. Metempsychosis ceased to be for Nerval a religious principle and became a principle of delirium and poetry. He dreamed passionately, obscurely, willfully exhausting the vision of a children's dance that appears so darkened and illuminated that it is accepted as an incomprehensible rite of some lost truth.

The tragic hero of antiquity, of the *chansons de geste*, and of the classical theater is abstemious of words, but Nerval, in pursuing the reality of language, pursued at the same time the reality of dreams. No modern poetry is more "narrative" than *Les Chimères*. The principle of illuminism penetrates the poems and the novel *Aurélia*. Illuminism is a belief in a personal enlightenment not accessible to mankind in general. Nothing ends, neither life nor death, because men and gods equally never cease being absorbed in the universe. The final substance of the sonnets—all the very simple words and the pauses between the words and the lines—is the only immobile element in Nerval's work. This substance, chained to the white pages, sings of perpetual becoming and recommencing where tragedy is an episode, where glory is a disappearance, where death is life.

Romanticism, of all the centuries and not solely of the nineteenth, is the dream of life, the harsh and provocative disproportion existing between imagined life and daily life. Rousseau, on certain pages of his *Rêveries*, bequeathed to the hypersensitive hearts of the nineteenth and twentieth centuries ways and exercises by which to attain the ecstasy of dreams. These romantics in their dream of life are today replaced by Gérard de Nerval in his life of dreams. The climate desired by Jean-Jacques was the dream of nature, but the climate desired by Nerval was the nature of dreams. The human solitude of Rousseau gave way to the mortal solitude of Nerval, who felt, more profoundly than the Swiss writer, the desert truth of the cosmos.

The love expressed by Nerval at the inception of the modern era is love of eternity, love of that force that bends trees and men, but that also straightens them up thanks to the indestructible truth of dreams. The poet Nerval knew himself as a living man and as a future dead man: he did not distinguish in himself the two roles, which are measured by the two rites of life and death. Uncrowned by life, this prince of Aquitania was crowned by death. It was fitting that at the birth of the theatrical romantic pessimism in the century that has given the greatest number of dreamers to the world, a single writer should cease contemplating from his real site the clouds of his dreams in order to live in his dream the transfigured image of his life.

El Desdichado

Nerval and Baudelaire, the two precursors of symbolism, and Mallarmé and Rimbaud, the two leading symbolist poets, are each represented by one text, one poem so often explored and analyzed by critics, so often memorized by readers, that it overshadows, unduly overshadows, the entire work: Nerval's *El Desdichado*, Baudelaire's *Correspondances*, Mallarmé's swan sonnet, and Rimbaud's *Bateau Ivre*. But there is good reason for this preference and emphasis. Especially in the case of Gérard de Nerval.

The Spanish title means "the disinherited," or the "alien," or the "ill-starred." *El desdichado* is the motto written on the shield of a mysterious knight in chapter 8 of Walter Scott's *Ivanhoe*. This knight is a wanderer who has lost his castle. The age of chivalry was always associated in Nerval's mind with his own ancestors. In a letter to George Sand (22 November 1853), he wrote that long ago he was a noble from the Midi: Gaston Phoebus d'Aquitaine. Genealogy was a cherished study for him, and in this sonnet he tells his history: what he once was and what he became.

Its date is uncertain, but it was first published in 1853, in *Le Mousquetaire*. His second bout with madness was in April 1853, when Nerval was forty-five. (The first serious attack was in 1841). He had just written *Sylvie*, which appeared in *La Revue des Deux Mondes* on 15 August 1853. *Aurélia* he wrote in 1854, the year that saw the end of his second crisis.

The sonnet's opening line, strong and forthright, condenses his life in three words:

> Je suis le Ténébreux,—le Veuf,—l'Inconsolé

> (I am the dark one, the widower, the unconsoled)

His psychic state has forced him to become an inhabitant of the night. Because of the darkness of his mind, he is a *ténébreux*. He is a widower (*veuf*) in the sense of having lost by death both Adrienne, the girl from the Valois castle who appeared in the children's dance, and Jenny Colon, the actress-singer he had loved. Nerval and Baudelaire were both attracted to Swedenborg's belief that all the women in a man's life are one woman, the spouse of an eternal marriage. In *Filles de Feu*, Nerval writes on "loving a nun in the form of an actress": *aimer une religieuse* (Adrienne) *sous la forme d'une actrice* (Jenny). The third term, *l'inconsolé*, may well stand for *inconsolable*—the man banished from ordinary happiness, *inconsolé*, a term by which Nerval identifies himself.

The second, very resonant line is a further identification and far more mysterious than the initial line:

> Le Prince d'Aquitaine à la Tour abolie.

> ([I am] the Prince of Aquitania whose tower is down.)

Nerval counted among his ancestors the Labrunie knights from Poitou, whose leader was called "le duc d'Aquitaine." The coat of arms of the Labrunie family was three silver towers, and the

Desdichado's coat of arms (in *Ivanhoe*) was an uprooted oak tree. Out of these two symbols Nerval forged one: a fallen tower, which might designate the ancestral castle that has disappeared, or the nobility of his family that has disappeared through successive marriages, or, in a more general sense, the loss of any connection with his paternal lands.

This line in the original French is used by Eliot in *The Waste Land*, part V, "What the Thunder Said." It is the end of the long poem whose protagonist is another *ténébreux*, another *déshérité*, robbed of his inheritance. Eliot's protagonist is speaking here of the decay of the land ("Here is no water but only rock"), of the two disciples meeting a mysterious stranger on the journey to Emmaus ("Who is the third who walks always beside you?"), and of the wanderer's approach to the Chapel Perilous in the Grail legend. The entire passage is dominated by the symbol of

> Falling towers
> Jerusalem Athens Alexandria
> Vienna London

The litany ends with the adjective *Unreal*, used earlier at the end of Part I, "The Burial of the Dead." Nerval's line about the tower that has collapsed follows Eliot's naming of his protagonist as the Fisher King in the Grail story:

> *I sat upon the shore*
> *Fishing . . .*

and his question of a disinherited king, not asked in Nerval:

> *Shall I at least set my lands in order?*

The tower, if erect, would symbolize sexual creative power, but also the power to govern the land and to govern oneself.

The last two lines of the quatrain recall the personal theme of love in the poet's life:

> *Ma seule étoile est morte,—et mon luth constellé*
> *Porte le soleil noir de la Mélancolie.*

> (My only *star* is dead,—and my constellated lute
> Wears the *black sun* of *Melancholy*.)

Each of the key words in these lines is both literal and symbolic. Nerval's two principal loves had died: Adrienne, the château girl who had become a religious, is "star" in the sense of redemption. Jenny, the actress, is a stage "star." The Tarot card, number 17, presents a star symbolizing a spiritual love.

The lute, so often associated with the poet-priest Orpheus, bears the reflection of "the black sun of Melancholy." This is an allusion to an event in April 1853, recorded by Nerval, that took place on the Place de la Concorde when he looked up at the dark sky of his religious beliefs and discovered that the sun and the stars had been extinguished. "Melancholy" is without much doubt the engraving of Albrecht Dürer, German painter of the sixteenth century, which shows a large female figure, angel of Melancholy, seated in the midst of scientific instruments. The medieval term "melancholy" in the sixteenth and seventeenth centuries referred to one of the four liquids in the human body that control man's temperament: blood, phlegm, bile, and melancholy. An excess of melancholy in the body was considered to be conducive to strange behavior and to suicide. (Hamlet was called the "melancholy Dane.")

With the second quatrain of the sonnet we move to Italy and to the vibrant memories of the English girl Octavie, whom Nerval met first in Marseille and then in Naples, and on a boat in the Bay of Naples. He encountered another girl in a religious shop in Naples, whom he calls *la brodeuse*, the embroiderer. When he saw her first, she was embroidering a flower on a religious vestment, presumably on a cope or a chasuble.

> *Dans la nuit du Tombeau, Toi qui m'as consolé,*
> *Rends-moi le Pausilippe et la mer d'Italie,*
> *La fleur qui plaisait tant à mon coeur désolé,*
> *Et la treille où le Pampre à la Rose s'allie.*

> (In the night of the tomb, you who consoled me,
> Give me back Posilippo and the sea of Italy,
> The *flower* that so delighted my desolate heart,
> And the trellis where the vine and the rose are entwined.)

Octavie was friendly and sympathetic. She consoled him when he spoke to her of ideas of suicide, but when his ardor became clear, she told him she had a fiancé in England. The Posilippo is an elevated spot near Naples that has a famous grotto. The legend claims that if you put your ear to the bottom of the grotto, you can hear voices from the underworld.

The *flower*, underlined in Nerval's text, is perhaps best explained by the flower being sewn with gold thread by the pious girl he observed and talked with in the Neapolitan shop. The sadness in his heart as he contemplated the flower is echoed in the last three syllables of *mélancolie*. *Une ancolie* is another word for *renoncule*, or buttercup. Gérard arranged a meeting with Octavie under a trellis in Portici, just outside Naples. The emblem of Portici is a vine branch and a rose. After calling himself "unconsoled" in line 1 of the sonnet, in line 5 he appears "consoled" (presumably by Octavie and *la brodeuse*, when the scene shifts from France to Italy, from Aquitaine to Posilippo). The extreme sentiments of consolation and desolation (*consolé* and *désolé*) are stated in the rhymes of the second quatrain and are of course the familiar contradictory pattern of human destiny especially apparent in madness. Nerval has the courage of a self-analyst as he delineates his life story. The creation of art is at the same time—and inevitably—a therapeutic exercise.

> *Suis-je Amour ou Phébus, Lusignan ou Biron?*

(Am I Love or Phoebus, Lusignan or Biron?)

This is a return to the two opening lines of the sonnet, in which Nerval pointedly reviews the problem of self-identification. Is he related to a figure in Greek mythology—to Cupid, the god of love and the son of Venus, or to Phoebus, who is Apollo, son of Jupiter and god of light and art? The other two names he questions are from his ancestral province, Le Poitou. Lusignan is a feudal family founded by Raymond Lusignan and Mélusine, a dragon-fairy figure. (Proust in his novel uses the name Mélusine to designate two of his characters: Gilberte, daughter of Swann, and Oriane, duchess of Guermantes.)

> *Mon front est rouge encor du baiser de la Reine.*

(My forehead is still red from the kiss of the queen.)

This magical, unforgettable moment in the poet's childhood, when Adrienne, at the end of the dance, kissed his forehead, would seem to initiate the lifelong quest for love, and at the same time, as in the previous line, the quest for self-identification. (This moment in a child's life is comparable to the moment during Marcel's carriage drive with Dr. Percepied in Combray, when he saw in a flash the three steeples of Martinville and Vieuxvicq.)

> *J'ai rêvé dans la Grotte où nage la Sirène . . .*

(I dreamed in the grotto where the siren swims . . .)

Many possible references are fused here in a seemingly simple line. The grotto of Posilippo and the siren Mélusine reappear in this possible review of literary memories: the grotto sirens of German poetry Nerval loved and translated.

> *Et j'ai deux fois vainqueur traversé l'Achéron:*
> *Modulant tour à tour sur la lyre d'Orphée*
> *Les soupirs de la Sainte et les cris de la Fée.*

(And twice a conqueror I crossed the Acheron:
Modulating alternately on the lyre of Orpheus
The sighs of the saint and the cries of the fairy.)

Traditionally, when at death a spirit crosses the Acheron, the first river of Hell, he is not able to return to the world. Twice Nerval crossed the bounds of sanity and successfully returned to the world of the sane. Here in the final tercet of the sonnet, the poet identifies himself with Orpheus descending to Hell to rescue Eurydice, and with Orpheus the poet, who accompanies himself on a lyre as he sings of the saint (possibly Adrienne or the embroiderer in Naples), and of the fairy—of Jenny, who played such parts on the stage, or of Mélusine, the girl-siren, founder of the Lusignan family.

Thus in fourteen lines, Nerval's life story is sketched—with references to key events and key obsessions. He presents himself as a man who is dispossessed, who has lost his loves, and who sings of those losses, a new Orpheus in the modern world who claims his derivation from Greece and the Middle Ages. At first reading, the sonnet may seem a medley of rich confusions. That is not the case: every detail is traceable and autobiographical. The style of this writing foreshadows the poetic process seventy years later of Eliot and Pound, and of Joyce in *Ulysses* and *Finnegans Wake*. The sonnet is a poetic transposition of a life, such as will be found in Eliot's *Four Quartets*. It only seems vague and mysterious and hermetic.

Nerval appears today as the precursor of all modern French poets.

He revived and revitalized the sonnet in his need to compress his search and suffering and dreams into a sentence or a quatrain. He was once an Aquitanian prince stripped of his castle and lands. In his wanderings he recalls the Bay of Naples, an unnamed flower, a trellis in Portici where a vine branch (Bacchus) joined with a rose (Venus). Among his ancestors was Lusignan, who lost his fairy-mermaid wife Mélusine. He survived death (or insanity) twice. He calls his beloved by at least five names in his sonnet: a star (*étoile*), a queen (*reine*), a siren (*sirène*), a saint (*sainte*), and a fairy (*fée*).

3

Charles Baudelaire: Time and the City

*A*fter more than a century, Charles Baudelaire appears today a classical writer—classical not simply in the sense that he is established and recognized and studied, but classical especially in his lucidity and power of analysis. In *Bénédiction* he speaks of the poet's *esprit lucide*. *Les Fleurs du Mal* (1857) occupies such a central position in the history of modern poetry because it satisfies this need for analysis and exploration of man's consciousness that the French have always demanded of their writers and even of their poets.

Baudelaire is classical also in the importance he places on the sense of order and architecture of a poem. One of the principal passions of the poet is the passion for order, for symmetry and structure. The writing of a poem is the discipline of form imposed upon emotion and experience and thought. Baudelaire professed an exalted belief in the willpower of the artist. "*Il n'y a pas de hasard dans l'oeuvre d'art*," he wrote in 1846.

The influence of this basic classicism of Baudelaire did not diminish during the symbolist period or during the past eighty years. Modern poetry presupposes a system of metaphysics. It affirms, first with Baudelaire and later with the philosophy of Henri Bergson, that the poet should place himself in the very center of what is real and merge his consciousness and sensibility with the universe. Whereas the Parnassian poet, in his description of the phenomena of the world, stayed within the domain of the real, the symbolist poet, taking Baudelaire as guide, tries to penetrate beyond the physical phenomena and reach what he calls the heart of reality.

All three terms—classicism, romanticism, and symbolism—have been applied to Baudelaire's art. The classical trait of this poet is represented in his longing for perfection, his lifelong striving to discover the ideal form of art and beauty. "Baudelairism" has become a frequently used term in modern criticism. It involves many matters: attitudes of the dandy, an attraction to the unhealthy and the morbid, habits of provocation and scorn. Baudelaire was essentially a man who felt the contradictions of his nature more acutely than most, who waged a spiritual struggle between the opposing forces of his greatness and his weakness, and who engaged his entire being in the adventure of poetry.

Upon the poet's death in 1867, his obituaries stressed sensational details in his life—his eccentricities, his diabolism, his dandyism. It is true that he lived the role of dandy in the Hôtel Lauzun on the Ile-Saint-Louis, that he often shocked the French bourgeoisie with his cynicism, that he cultivated an attitude toward satanism and the Gothic tale or *roman noir*. But today, thanks to the accessibility of all his writings, we know that far more important than his exterior appearance and behavior was the "inner dandyism" of his spirit. Baudelaire is the first modern poet because of his awareness of disorder in the world and in himself. Satanism is at the center of his work, not by histrionic black-magic values, but by the poet's horror of man's fate and his obsession with guilt. The pathology of Baudelaire's sadomasochism has been elaborately studied in recent years.

When Baudelaire was writing his earliest poems, about 1845, his principal references and directions came from romanticism. He felt close affinity with the enthusiasm of Gautier and Banville, with the esoteric interests of Nerval, with the macabre audacities of Pétrus Borel. These men, more than the leaders of the romantic movement—Hugo, Lamartine, Vigny—helped him define modern poetry by its secrecy, its spirituality, its aspiration toward the infinite. He was among the first to define romanticism as a way of feeling (*une manière de sentir*). The example of Delacroix, Poe, and Wagner, as well as the more philosophical Swedenborg and Joseph de Maistre, confirmed the intuition of Baudelaire concerning the modern form of melancholy and nostalgia. In his search for beauty through the *forêts de symboles*, where every element is hieroglyph, he practiced the art of symbolism instinctively long before it reached its consecration in theory and manifesto.

For many Americans, Baudelaire is still the French poet who was influenced by Poe and who exaggerated the importance of Poe. He recognized himself in the American poet. He translated Poe because of their common traits: hysteria, which often replaced the free functioning of the will; a lack of harmony between the nervous tensions and the intellect; a scorn for the concept of progress and for the materialism of their century; a love for the suggestiveness of dreams. The psychological analyses of Laclos, the prose style of Chateaubriand, and the philosophy of Joseph de Maistre probably exerted a far deeper influence on Baudelaire than any aspect of Poe's writings. But the American poet had for the Frenchman the power of a myth, and the particular significance that Baudelaire found in Poe was to play an important role in the development of Mallarmé's genius and Valéry's.

At the time of *Les Fleurs du Mal*, philosophers had been humbled in the presence of the positivistic scientists. Baudelaire's revelation of poetry revindicated belief in the spiritual destiny of man. His example and his art convinced his readers that man has the right to ask of poetry the solution to the problems of human destiny. The Parnassians created a purely descriptive art of exterior concrete objects. Baudelaire's revelation was to provide a metaphysical conception of the same universe. His famous sonnet on synesthesia and symbolism, *Correspondances*, reassigns to the poet his ancient role of *vates*, of soothsayer, who by his intuition of the concrete, of immediately perceived things, is led to the *idea* of these things, to the intricate system of "correspondences."

The sonnet was to become the principal key to symbolism as defined by subsequent poets. Already, for Baudelaire, nature was a word, an allegory. To the poet is revealed *une ténébreuse et profonde unité*, which is the unison of the sensible and spiritual universes. The experience of the poet is the participation of all things invading him, with their harmonies and analogies. They bear the sign of the First Word, of their original unity.

In *L'Albatros*, one of his most frequently anthologized poems, Baudelaire projects the story of his personal drama. The poet is caught by the world as the albatross is caught on the deck of a ship. His large wings, the source of his strength and beauty in the air, make it impossible for him to rise when he is placed on the deck. Baudelaire turns the drama into an almost comic picture of frustration. This personal tragedy of the poet far outdistances the lesser conflicts in

Baudelaire's life: the endless arguments with his mother; the long, more than twenty-five-year liaison with Jeanne Duval; his constant quarrels with creditors and notaries; his struggles with a hostile press.

The elements of pathos in the poems are so universal and so humble that we can easily fraternize with this poet as we read of the indefinable sadness of a large city, the dreams and idealizations of a drunkard, the heart of an old servant woman. Whatever can be called metaphysical suffering in Baudelaire is so joined with daily anguish of the most commonplace kind that one illuminates the other and provides an experience of warmth and love.

Baudelaire has been psychoanalyzed, first by a doctor, René Laforgue, and more recently by Jean-Paul Sartre. But before those writers, he psychoanalyzed himself and derived a principle that psychoanalysis has extolled: the principle of compensation: "Tout mystique a un vice caché" (Every mystic has a hidden vice).

His childhood love, his intense love for his mother, "*le vert paradis des amours enfantines*" (the green paradise of childish love), never left his thoughts for long. This carefully protected memory of early happiness led him to write that poetry is "childhood willfully recovered" (*l'enfance retrouvée à volontée*). Baudelaire defined genius as *l'enfance nettement formulée* (childhood lucidly formulated).

School after school of poets has chosen objects that seemed at the time distinctive and privileged. School after school of poets favored chains and fires of love, the blushing dagger, compendious oceans (to designate tears). Hugo and the romantics chose twilight, stars, meadows. The emblems of Mallarmé and the symbolists were vases, swans, jewels. Baudelaire described a world as unpoetic, in the traditional sense, as possible: skeletons, cemeteries, barracks, hovels, prostitutes, gamblers, clowns. His art involved the creation of their beauty. These words were related to his personal experience, which was undeniably an experience in pessimism. Baudelaire held a distinct distaste for the advocates of optimism, for those who denied the existence of evil or who justified it, or for those who dissimulated it under concepts of evolution and racial perfectibility. In distinguishing himself from those advocates, Baudelaire became the poet and the thinker of our age, of what we like to call "modernity."

Paris

Charles Baudelaire was born in Paris in 1821, the year of Napoleon's death. At the age of twenty-one, independent of his mother and stepfather, and thanks to a small inheritance, he lived the life of a dandy, of the youthful artist intoxicated with ambition and power. He took his place beside a few other fervent spirits for whom the writing of poetry was a sacred mission: Banville, Gautier, Nerval. A strange sea voyage of nine months (June 1841 to February 1842) had taken Baudelaire away from Paris. On his return he saw the city more clearly, saw more lucidly the many ways in which Paris was changing:

> *La forme d'une ville*
> *Change plus vite, hélas, que le coeur d'un mortel.*

> (The form of a city
> Changes faster, alas, than the heart of a mortal.)

It was a world of parvenus and an enriched bourgeoisie. Stores now had tall glass windows and were illuminated. Streets were covered with macadam, and sidewalks had been installed for the first time. Gaslight at night had drastically altered the habits of the city, the nocturnal life of the boulevards and the theaters. The development of railroads was only one aspect of a new life of luxury and pleasure.

This was the moment when Charles Baudelaire inherited 75,000 francs, and momentarily thought in terms of a noble destiny, of a life that would be lived in alliance with beauty, in accordance with the dream of a superior dandy. He lived successively on the Quai de Béthune, on the rue Vaneau, and on the Ile-Saint-Louis in the Hôtel Pimodan, which was the first choice of residence for the Bohemian princes of the day. He cultivated the attitude of detachment and indifference. As a member of *la bohême dorée* (the gilded bohemian life), which included such figures as Gautier and Nerval, Baudelaire tried by means of art and artifice to correct all natural imperfections, all imperious instincts. Nature was the original sin in his creed of a dandy: *Ce qui est naturel est abominable* (What is natural is abominable).

The new types of the period were being observed by the writers and the artists, as they emerged and distinguished themselves by speech and dress: *le garde national*, for example, *le concierge, la lorette* (courtesan). The artists in particular, a Gavarni and a Daumier, and the apprentice artist, called *un rapin*, were quick to seize upon the comic trait and underscore it. Joseph Prudhomme, a character of the novelist Monnier, an example of bourgeois narrow-mindedness, was the real enemy of the artist and the dandy. Joseph Prudhomme and the pharmacist Homais in Flaubert's *Madame Bovary* stupidly believed in the concept of progress. On this score, Baudelaire's vituperations were ferocious. In countless aphorisms, he flailed the doctrine of progress as being a deceit, a vast dupery. In his role of dandy writer he was determined to avoid all sentimentality, all facility in writing, all turgid use of common sense. What attracted him, what he insisted on cultivating in himself, was a new form of beauty characterized by the strange, the bizarre, the abnormal. Dandyism permitted Baudelaire to scoff and blaspheme. He thereby affirmed a bond with some of the archromantic heroes of a generation or two earlier: Goethe's Werther, Chateaubriand's René, Byron's Manfred.

There are passions peculiar to each period. Baudelaire looked upon the heroes of Balzac, a Vautrin and a Rastignac whose passions are explicable by the social condition of the Restoration, as comparable to the heroes of the *Iliad*. The heroes of Paris represent the new human drives, in harmony with their age, but the power and drama of those drives have as much beauty and universal significance as those in heroes of other centuries.

Baudelaire is the modern poet in the fullest sense who rediscovered for poetry its real destiny. The goal of poetry is itself, its own intrinsic beauty. As the Greeks once taught, poetry is a delectation for the spirit, a ravishment of the soul. Whereas Théophile Gautier tended to restrict and limit the poet's role in making him a prisoner of appearances, in turning him into a spectator of the visible world of objects and landscapes and animals, Baudelaire became the *voyant*, the seer looking for and finding the meaning of things. Gautier was a sculptor in words, who built up pictures with words. But Baudelaire was a singer, a magician who was dissatisfied with his verses unless they possessed an incantatory power.

At the age of eighteen, Baudelaire began to take possession of Paris, to see the city in its multiple aspects of horror and beauty. He was no Rastignac whose will was to conquer the city. He had none of the dangerous exuberance of the Balzac hero, none of the overpowering drive to exploit the city for his own material gains. Far more complex than the provincial Eugène de Rastignac, Charles Baudelaire was a native Parisian whose curiosity about vice became a mode of investigation, and essentially an investigation of himself. During the early years, everything led him back to the poems he was writing, to the book he was planning to publish eventually. The themes of his work, which may seem limited, had so many variations that behind the apparent sterility he spoke of so often, the creative sterility, there was a real fecundity. Every walk he took along the Seine and in the streets of Paris furnished him with images he was to use in his poems and prose poems. No book is more a quintessence of life, a condensation of life, than *Les Fleurs du Mal* (1857). The art offered to him by the city often became the source of his poem: a painting of Delacroix inspired *Don Juan aux Enfers*, a statue of Ernest Christophe inspired *Le Masque*, a drawing of an unknown artist inspired *Une Martyre*. Literature was also used: a line of Gérard de Nerval is at the genesis of *Voyage à Cythère*. Slight incidents counted too: the sound of wood being chopped in a courtyard is recorded in *Chant d'Automne*.

Chant d'Automne, one of the most solemn canticles of Baudelaire, is a supreme example of his art, where there is no narrative, no preaching, no doctrine, where every line is a condensation of an impassioned man. Pure passion without sentimentality. In the opening stanza

> *Bientôt nous plongerons dans les froides ténèbres:*
> *Adieu, vive clarté de nos étés trop courts:*
> *J'entends déjà tomber avec des chocs funèbres,*
> *Le bois retentissant sur le pavé des cours.*

> (Soon we will plunge into the cold dark:
> Farewell, strong light of our too brief summers:
> I hear already falling with funereal thuds,
> The resounding wood on the pavement of the courts.)

time is materialized in the pieces of wood resounding as they strike against the pavement. We are in between the violent seasons of the year: summer with its brightness and the cold gloom of winter. The falling wood beats out the seconds of time. This sound, which marks the passing of time, announces death, at the end of time, and the opening verb; *nous plongerons*, announces the dizzying plunge of the poet into the cold of winter, which is the cold of death.

The entire poem is the moment of pause on the brink of a great change. After the intense life and light of summer will come, swiftly, almost with the close of the poem, the opposite experience, of cold and immobility. Winter is far more than a season; it is the symbol of growing old, the sign of the drying up of energy and life. The logs of wood that fall, *chaque bûche qui tombe*, expand into the full dimensions of metaphors. They are the minutes that tick by,

the beating of the heart, and they evoke the gallows and the battering ram in its act, causing a tower to collapse. The poet's mind is
so obsessed with death that the repetitive sounds he hears come
from the nailing of a coffin, and he wonders for whom the coffin is
being built. Death is the most mysterious of all departures, and the
sound of the echoing wood has something of that mystery:

> *Ce bruit mystérieux sonne comme un départ.*

This coffin, in its metaphorical power, represents the burial of more
than one thing: of summer perhaps, of youth, of the poet himself, of
time. This autumn song is the synchronization of many elements.
The sun shining on the sea is so brief an experience for the poet that
it calls up the images of death: the setting sun and the tomb waiting
for the end. Each word in the poem is a part of the whole, in the
same way that autumn involves the summer that preceded it and the
winter that is to follow. A log being cut in a Paris courtyard for a
fireplace becomes the gallows, and a battering ram, and a coffin. The
poet's obsession has found a word, a sign, capable of depicting it.

   Paris is both real for Baudelaire and endlessly changing. He sees
it and he sees beyond it because it is fertile in its power to stir his
imagination. In the second edition of *Les Fleurs du Mal*, of 1861, a
new section appeared, called *Tableaux parisiens*, of which *Le Cygne* is
perhaps Baudelaire's major piece on Paris. It is dedicated to Victor
Hugo, who at the time of publication was in exile from Paris. Exile is
the principal theme of the poem, and Paris is the city that stimulates
the poet's fertile memory of exiles. He is crossing the new Carrousel,
an esplanade constructed in the Second Empire, situated between
the Louvre and the Tuileries. Baudelaire is thinking of one of the
famous exiles of antiquity: Andromache, a captive in the palace of
Pyrrhus, and exiled from Troy and the river Simois, beside which she
lamented Hector's death. The poem opens with her name

> *Andromaque, je pense à vous!*

> (Andromache, I am thinking of you!)

and ends with the word *captifs* and a general reference to all those
who suffer in humiliating captivity.

Je pense
Aux captifs, aux vaincus . . .

(I am thinking
Of men in captivity, of men vanquished . . .)

The poem celebrates the deepening power of Baudelaire's psychic experience. In his walk near the Louvre, in a section of the city where some demolition work is going on and débris is everywhere, he invokes the solemn majesty of Andromache weeping beside the ridiculously small Simois. The Paris spot was once the site of a menagerie, and the poet recalls a poignantly dramatic incident he had once observed there: a swan, having escaped from its cage, was dragging its white plumage in the dust of a dried-up gutter. It turned its head toward the sky as if it reproached God for not sending rain. The swan was in exile from its native lake, as Andromache was in exile from the Trojan Simois. A queen and a bird both testify to the strange, fatal myth of exile that preoccupies and disturbs the poet as he walks through Paris, the city that alters its appearance faster than the heart of a man changes his fidelities.

The opening of the second part of *Le Cygne*, stanza 8, recapitulates the first part by stating again the changes in the city and the steadfastness of the poet's sadness:

Paris change! mais rien dans ma mélancolie
N'a bougé.

(Paris changes! but nothing in my sadness
Has moved.)

The city itself has become the myth. This myth, everything that the city suggests, has become more concrete than the buildings, those that stand and those that are partly demolished.

Tout pour moi devient allégorie.

(Everything becomes allegory for me.)

The thought of exile, with which the poem opened, like a vibrant chord of music,

Andromaque, je pense à vous!

has become more real and more solid than the granite of the buildings in the real landscape.

> *Et mes chers souvenirs sont plus lourds que des rocs.*

(And my dear memories are heavier than rocks.)

The transformation is now total: the swan returns with its vain movements, and Andromache bends over an empty tomb she has constructed for a funeral offering. By association, another vision rises up—that of a black girl walking through the mud and fog of the northern city and trying to see the coconut trees of Africa that are not there.

> *Je pense à la négresse,*
> *Piétinant dans la boue, et cherchant*
> *Les cocotiers absents de la superbe Afrique.*

(I think of the black girl,
Walking in the mud, and searching for
The absent coconut trees of proud Africa.)

These memories grow in such strength and pervasiveness that Paris, in the final stanza of the poem, becomes a forest and the memories become the piercing notes of a hunting horn:

> *Un vieux Souvenir sonne à plein souffle du cor!*

(An old memory rings out a full blast of the horn!)

This forest is the poet's exile:

> *Ainsi dans la forêt où mon esprit s'exile.*

(Thus in the forest where my spirit is exiled.)

The list of imaginary exiles in *Le Cygne*—Andromache, the swan, the black girl—concludes with the poet as the exile in Paris. But in a theological sense, all mankind, all men are in exile. The allegory of the city is all-inclusive, and the great exiled writers have testified to this: Dante, Joyce, Claudel, Saint-John Perse. Baudelaire in Paris is exiled from it by the power of transformation. The images in his memory expand as the real Paris around him contracts. He remembers a world more real than the real world. Before Mallarmé, Baudelaire is the poet of absences. In abolishing the exterior world, he substitutes for it: the native lake of the swan, Africa of the black girl, the empty tomb of Hector. The poem narrates the poet's walk across the Place du Carrousel and a voyage through his memory.

This same kind of transformation takes place in *Rêve parisien*, where the city is idealized into a palace of metal and marble and water, from which all vegetation has been abolished. Paris is Babel, and the poet is the architect of this dream world. In the *spleen* sonnet that begins *Pluviôse, irrité contre la ville entière* (Pluvius, irritated with the entire city), Paris and the poet's room are the site of transformations and substitutions: the dead in the cemetery receive the rain, implied in such a word as *Pluviôse*; the soul of a dead poet walks as if alive along the rooftops; a bell has the human characteristic of a lament; a smoking log wheezes like a human; the Jack of Hearts and the Queen of Spades in a dirty pack of cards engage in a sinister conversation concerning their former passion. In such a poem, life and death are seen as merged or confused. Inanimate objects are animated and given human characteristics. The transformation involving matter and spirit is phantasmagoria.

Baudelaire and Eliot

The poet is a wayfarer, an intercessor, an intermediary, because of whom we are able to feel related to forces that surpass our minds. Because of the poet, the universe perceived by our senses—seasons and cities, men and their wretchedness—is loved attentively and fervently and knowingly. Charles Baudelaire, a century after his death, remains one of our witnesses.

Toward the middle of the nineteenth century, Baudelaire was representative of a certain number of elements that the spiritual makeup of France did not possess at that time, and that, since Baudelaire's age, have been studied and explored with an ever-renewed critical acumen. Every page of his writings celebrates the imagination as man's noblest faculty. Baudelaire possessed the indispensable gift for the writing of poetry: the analysis, the lucidity, and the affirmation of the self. He nurtured the impassioned plan to rediscover authentic human values and to oppose those forms of stagnation that in each generation man invents for his own misery.

Baudelaire was never a militant member of any group. Somewhat distant and somewhat secretive, but with an intellectual firmness that caused him to be respected and even feared, he studied problems that have dominated the critical conscience and poetic creativity in Europe and America during the past one hundred years. His art represents an awareness of man's situation in the modern world, and his example has taught subsequent poets that it is necessary to find a new language, a language adequate to transmit the feelings of modern man. The poet's first obligation is to create a language that is his, in order not to lose his identity of a poet.

The period of time beginning with Baudelaire's career as a poet and extending to today is a century of European and American civilization, of which the principal characteristic is, according to Baudelaire and to some contemporary poets, notably T. S. Eliot, disorder. Disorder in every domain. Baudelaire was the initiator of a significant attitude, an outlook on the disorder he saw everywhere. He was also the initiator of a way of feeling, a way of understanding disorder. For he was, at the dawn of modern poetry, the writer who claimed that all first-rate poetry is preoccupied with morality. If Baudelaire discovered for himself certain religious values—humility, for example, the need for prayer, the notion of original sin—his obligation as a poet was not to practice Christianity as a religion but to make its necessity felt in the modern world.

The initial impulse of poetry is the emotion the poet feels in his relationship with himself, in his relationship with others, with the world around him, and also with his past, with childhood, with the dead. This theme is central in Baudelaire, as it is also in Eliot, who tells us at the end of *Little Gidding*:

> We are born with the dead
> · · · · · · · · · · · · · · ·
> The moment of the rose and the moment of the yew tree
> Are of equal duration.

The poet's work is truly the quest and exploration of the past. In examining certain works of art, Baudelaire wrote that he often experienced a vision of the childhood of the artist. In one sentence in particular, he announces a principle associated today with Proust, concerning a child's sorrow, which, when enlarged, may become in the adult of a marked sensitivity the foundation of a work of art: "*Tel petit chagrin, telle jouissance de l'enfant démesurément grossis par une exquise sensibilité deviennent plus tard dans l'homme adulte, même à son insu, le principe d'une oeuvre d'art"* ("A small sorrow, a small pleasure of the child, exaggeratedly enlarged by a exquisite sensibility, become later in the adult male, even unknown to him, the principle of a work of art"). This passage, of great importance for Baudelaire's aesthetics, ends with the celebrated formula: "Genius is childhood distinctly formulated" (*Le génie n'est que l'enfance nettement formulée*).

Baudelaire's greatness is in the degree of intensity to which he elevated poetic imagery. His renovation of poetic language was accompanied by a renovation of his attitude toward life. In his aesthetics, the slightest object may be magnified by the poet. He taught that there is poetry and beauty in the most trivial aspects of modern life: a swan escaping from its cage and dragging its white plumage through the dust of the street; an old man walking down a city street; a multitude of people deadened by pleasure . . .

It would be possible to write a study on the close relationship between the prolonged metaphor of Baudelaire, in which the idea and the image are miraculously fused (*La chevelure*, for example), and the "objective correlative" of Eliot, or between the image capable of translating and supporting a significant human experience and the "memory-sensation" of Proust, that sensorial experience that permits a man to recover a feeling by which he was once animated. Eliot, in *Ash Wednesday* and *Four Quartets*, and Marcel, listening to Vinteuil's music, or tasting a madeleine dipped in tea, rediscover places and privileged moments. They are nontemporal moments. A century earlier, Baudelaire, in *Le Balcon*, had announced the principle of that mnemonic art:

> *Je sais l'art d'évoquer les minutes heureuses*
> *Et revis mon passé blotti dans tes genoux.*

> (I know the art of evoking the happy minutes
> And I see again my past smothered in your knees.)

Time recalled is not time for Eliot:

> Time present and time past
> . . . .
> What might have been and what has been
> Point to one end, which is always present.
>
> *(Burnt Norton)*

The happiness that invades Marcel as he drinks the cup of tea makes of him a being freed from contingencies: he ceases being accidental and even mediocre. This is exactly what Baudelaire had said in the last stanza of *Le Balcon*, in the form of an interrogation:

> *Ces serments, ces parfums, ces baisers infinis*
> *Renaîtront-ils d'un gouffre interdit à nos sondes?*

> (Will those promises, those perfumes, those infinite kisses
> Be reborn from a depth forbidden to our soundings?)

Proust in Paris and Eliot in London discovered almost at the same time a Baudelairian principle concerning time and the way in which a writer interprets time. Baudelaire, in translating the feeling of spleen, had said:

> *J'ai plus de souvenirs que si j'avais mille ans.*

> (I have more memories than if I were a thousand years old.)

And Proust, in *Le Temps Retrouvé*, says in one of his most profound sentences:

> *Une heure n'est pas qu'une heure, c'est un vase rempli*
> *de parfums, de sons, de projets et de climats!*

> (An hour is not merely an hour, it is a vase filled
> with perfumes, sounds, projects, and climates.)

And Eliot, in his fervent meditation on time, says at the end of *Burnt Norton*:

> Even while the dust moves
> There rises the hidden laughter
> Of children in the foliage,
> Quick now, here, now, always—
> Ridiculous the waste sad time
> Stretching before and after.

The artist is the man who narrates himself and at the same time narrates the customs of his contemporaries. When the writer tells his dreams, his fantasies, his loves, he is telling the dreams, fantasies, and loves of other men. To be the interpreter of his age is a first duty for the poet, but it is not a comfortable duty when the poet is embittered by the ugliness of contemporary life. The meaning of history is indispensable for the man who wants to remain a poet. The meaning of history is also the meaning of myths, the meaning of antiquity. Eliot, in *The Waste Land*, underscores the parallelism between the contemporary event and the myths of antiquity. It is the principal procedure used by Joyce in *Ulysses*. And Baudelaire, in his major poem on Paris, the city where everything changes, when he sees a swan escaped from its cage, thinks of the great exiled figures of history, and especially of

> *Andromaque, des bras d'un grand époux tombée,*
> *Auprès d'un tombeau vide en extase courbée.*

> (Andromache, fallen from the arms of a great spouse,
> Bent in ecstasy close to an empty tomb.)

The overture section of *The Waste Land*, "The Burial of the Dead," has four verses that evoke London today:

> Unreal City,
> Under the brown fog of a winter dawn,
> A crowd flowed over London Bridge, so many,
> I had not thought death had undone so many.

Eliot himself in his notes gives the two sources of this passage: the third canto of Dante's *Inferno*:

> *si lunga tratta di gente*
> (such a long train of people)

and the Baudelaire poem, *Les sept vieillards*, which begins:

> *Fourmillante cité, cité pleine de rêves,*
> *Où le spectre en plein jour raccroche le passant.*

> (Swarming city, city full of dreams,
> Where the ghost in full daylight grabs hold of the passerby.)

Baudelaire's poem is a walk through the streets of Paris, and during this walk the city becomes the setting for an eruption of demonic forces. The city takes on a human form. Baudelaire calls it a colossus (*un colosse puissant*). At the beginning of the poem, where the narrow streets (*les canaux étroits*) become arteries, the circulatory system of the giant, the reality of the exterior, is destroyed. The city loses its shape and the old man coming into the vision of the poet is seen as hostile to the universe. This *sinistre vieillard* is doubled and multiplied. The one real action in this part of the city, shaken by the noise of the tumbril carts, is an inner satanic action taking place in the poet's imagination.

In the composition of *The Waste Land*, the poet incorporates this expansion of reality, of which Dante and Baudelaire had been, according to Eliot, the principal artisans. In his first essay on the French poet, Eliot writes, "All first-rate poetry is occupied with morality: this is the lesson of Baudelaire." The phantom city, "Unreal City," is the first city that Baudelaire had sung of in *Les sept vieillards, cité pleine de rêves* ("The seven old men, City Full of Dreams"), and then Dante's vestibule (canto 3), where we see those dead who had led a perfectly neutral life. The judgment of the world in "The Burial of the Dead" is very harsh, and the poet does not exclude himself from this judgment. The passage ends with a line of Baudelaire:

> . . . *hypocrite lecteur!—mon semblable—mon frère!*

> (. . . hypocrite reader!—my twin—my brother!)

The verse, quoted in French in Eliot's text, evokes more clearly than a translation could have done the theme of modern ennui, which is the central subject of the poem *Au lecteur*. Ennui, called by Baudelaire the ugliest of our vices, explains the atmosphere of *The Waste Land*, the mournful, neutralized atmosphere that comes from a universe of evil, and even from the diabolical universe of *Les sept vieillards*.

Eliot's arid earth, the hardened, calcined reign from which all life has been withdrawn,

> And the dry stone no sound of water,

was called by Baudelaire in *Un voyage à Cythère*,

Un désert rocailleux troublé par des cris aigres.

(A rocky desert disturbed by bitter cries.)

Whether it is Baudelaire's Paris of the swan escaping from its cage, or the sinister old man, or the London of Eliot and the crowd on London Bridge,

And each man fixed his eyes before his feet

whether it is the *désert rocailleux* of *Cythère* or "this stony rubbish" of *The Waste Land*, the poet's art is the use of the sensible world. The two poets speak of the death inherent in each life, but especially of the spiritual death of modern man. The poet renders this present sterility, thanks to the poetic process, which Baudelaire called *sortilège*, or *sorcellerie évocatoire*.

Eliot saw in Baudelaire the example of a writer for whom criticism and poetry are converging aspects of the same literary process. The books of each one represent the search for a form of analysis capable of translating the consciousness of an objective work, when it is a question of criticism. Whether it is a poem or a critical essay, the definitive result recapitulates a personal reaction in which the intelligence of the writer and his sensibility are similarly engaged.

Baudelaire's "*Le Voyage*" and Eliot's "Gerontion" are poems that can be explained in terms of a cultural context. For Baudelaire, the world has become so small that it is reduced to what a single man sees, to the image of the inner life of a man:

Amer savoir, celui qu'on tire d'un voyage!
Le monde, monotone et petit, aujourd'hui,
Hier, demain, toujours, nous fait voir notre image . . .

(Bitter knowledge we draw from a voyage!
The world, monotonous and small, today,
Yesterday, tomorrow, always, makes us see our image . . .)

The same motifs of time, of consciousness of evil, and of spacial and chronological ambiguities are to be found in "Gerontion":

> After such knowledge, what forgiveness? Think now
> History has many cunning passages . . .

These two poems are so deeply rooted in the meaning of a historical period that they defy any ordinary analysis. Baudelaire's voyager is the man who sets out for the pure joy of leaving his familiar world, and he is also the child who does not leave, who is in love with maps and pictures:

> *l'enfant amoureux de cartes et d'estampes.*

(the child in love with maps and prints)

The character in Eliot's poem,

> An old man in a draughty house,

finds it difficult to return to former experiences and to comprehend them. But the minds of Eliot's old man and of Baudelaire's voyager contain the universe. There is a moment at the end of each poem when the protagonist experiences the intoxication and exaltation of the infinite:

> . . . Gull against the wind, in the windy straits
> Of Belle Isle . . .

> *Nos coeurs que tu connais sont remplis de rayons!*

(Our hearts which you know are filled with rays!)

Each of these poets has sung of the aridity of contemporary life, and each one also has sung of the same aspiration toward purity, the same search for humility. Each offers the example of the creative and the critical intelligence. In reading the measured verses of these two poets we become accomplices of extreme sentiments. This poetry does not reassure us. It does not engulf us with illusions.

There are many themes common to Baudelaire and Eliot: the strong attraction to the sea, an obsession with the city and its populous neighborhoods, spleen, a tone of derision, and especially the theme of anguish, comparable to the anguish studied by Jean-Paul Sartre in *La Nausée*. There is still to be studied an art, specifically

Baudelairian, that Eliot learned from the French poet and perfected in accordance with his own aptitude and talent. It is the art of evoking a memory, and often a distant memory, deliberately and willfully, the art of associating the sensation of this memory with the spirit and the intellect, and at the same time excluding all sentimentality.

In the specific pages on Paris and in many other pages throughout his work, Baudelaire reveals an attraction to the exaggerated and the absolute, a taste for the extreme, which is not central in the French tradition. The directions in poetry proposed by *Les Fleurs du Mal* were followed by Rimbaud and Mallarmé, and somewhat later by Valéry in France and by Eliot in England. These directions included a renewal of classical form in poetry. As a meticulous craftsman, Baudelaire opposed the ancient concept of inspiration and the verbal prolixity that romanticism permitted. In keeping with the classical tradition of a Racine, the formal aspects of Baudelaire's art are severe and simple, and the universe within the poems is extreme in its depiction of the irreparable, the irremediable, remorse, horror, death, nightmares, assassinations.

In his will to extract beauty from evil (*les fleurs du mal*), Baudelaire first gave the impression of a will to scandalize and shock. This was true in only the most superficial sense, and Théophile Gautier, in his preface to *Les Fleurs du Mal*, as early as 1868, defended Baudelaire against the reproach that the work was bizarre and original in a histrionic sense. Baudelaire's descent into himself does not appear today as a search for the abnormal or the unusual, but rather as a search for his childhood, for that indestructible purity in terms of which he saw all the later catastrophes and failures: his illness, the censorship of some of the poems, his abortive attempts to enter the Académie Française. The sensibility of a child in its lucidity and poignancy, the fleeting sadness of a childhood experience—these, for Baudelaire, became later principles of his art. *Le vert paradis* of his earliest loves was a world intact and inexhaustible, from which the poet could always efficaciously construct and impose an imaginary world on the real world of Paris.

Baudelaire's greatest love was for what he believed he had lost: the innocence of his childhood, and his strongest sentiment of hate was for that form of evil that had deprived him of happiness: *l'obscur Ennemi qui nous ronge le coeur* (the dark enemy who gnaws at our heart).

Brunetière's indictment of Baudelaire as the poet extolling de-
bauchery and immorality illustrates the attitude of most of the first
critics. Such a thesis seems today in direct contradiction to the real
meaning and spirit of the book: the antagonism between good and
evil, that spiritual and physical struggle implicit in the subtitle of
the longest section of the book: *spleen et idéal*. The meaning of such
a poem as *La Charogne* is not in the revolting picture of putrefaction
but in the biblical warning that the body of man is but dust and
returns to dust: *pulvis es*.

In the major lyric tradition of France, the language of Baudelaire
bears a strong resemblance to that of Ronsard and Racine and Hugo,
but as a poet, in the subject matter of his book, he waged, far
more desperately than they did, an uninterrupted struggle with the
nothingness of man, with that part of us that at all times is seeking
to annihilate life.

That particular struggle was Baudelaire's life struggle, and all the
major aspects of his biography are related to it. No poet, unless it
was Villon, was more attached to Paris than Baudelaire, and yet no
poet was less nationalistic than Baudelaire. Paris was the city for
him, the only city, but he made it into the site of his personal
struggle in which he recapitulated the oldest tragedy of man, the
humblest of all tragedies: the combat between the greatness of his
mind and aspiration and the fatal weakness of his will, where the
daily routine of suffering and humiliation won out.

The key to Baudelaire's book is the meaning he gives to the word
evil: les fleurs du mal. What is evil for him? This is the hardest
question to answer concerning Baudelaire, and the most important.
It may be possible to reach this answer by considering the trait that,
more than any other, distinguishes Baudelaire's temperament: his
despair. As in the case of Dante, whose tendency to anger is somewhat explained by his pride, by his certainty of Paradise, and by
the triumph of a just and loving God, so Baudelaire's tendency to
despair may be explained by his disgust for himself, by his feeling
that a world was collapsing around him, by his experience of a
suffering God. Evil, then, for Baudelaire, would be his consciousness of the world, his ever-present awareness of the physical forces
around him that lead to change and destruction and annihilation.

But everything is difficult to define in Baudelaire, because everything is complex in the modern sense: his sentiment of love as well
as his experience of despair. Some of his greatest poems are surely
his love poems, and they are different from the love poems of other
French poets. Whether it is to Jeanne he is speaking, or to Marie,

or to la Présidente, or to his mother, Baudelaire is concerned with some totally complex form of desire that grows and deepens in him as his fear of being satisfied grows and deepens. Baudelaire is the most chaste of the love poets. In his garden of evil, he contemplates the flowers, smells their perfumes, and condemns them. The very greatness and limitlessness of passion turns him away from it and converts him into a solitary figure who feels indulgent toward very few beings in the world, and toward very few works of art.

The creation of art was his life. The labor he spent on rewriting and perfecting his verses was his search for the absolute and his morality. He believed that genius has to sever the connection with the norm. The pain of living and the desire to live became identical to Baudelaire. The barrenness of life was insufferable for him. Some form of ornamentation is therefore indispensable. Poetry is the loftiest form of ornamentation because its beauty is metaphysics. In such a simple title as *Paradis artificiels*, Baudelaire states his creed as a poet. The need for ornamentation is the same as the need for escape. Exoticism and erotism are both inexhaustible for Baudelaire, and they both have to do with the inner life and the former life (*vie intérieure* and *vie antérieure*): deserts, passion, the tropics, desires, oceans, and oases.

As Dante was supremely concentrated on dogma, so Baudelaire was supremely concentrated on his inner life. His attitude of nonchalance and indifference was exterior. At the dawn of modern poetry, slightly more than one hundred years ago, Baudelaire refined his instincts and thoughts by meditation. In speaking directly to his reader, Baudelaire, for the first time in French poetry, threatened to curse him if he did not show him pity:

> *Plains-moi, sinon, je te maudis!*

> (Pity me! Otherwise, I curse you!)

Eliot did not wait for eternity "in order to change into himself." His voice and the expression on his face, as well as his work, testified, during the last years of his life, to certain ways of thinking and feeling that are usually associated with a classical writer, with a man who already occupies his place in the history of letters and the history of civilization.

The slightly transformed line of Mallarmé I have just used was first applied to the American Poe, whom Eliot perhaps would not have read so attentively if Baudelaire had not revealed him to

French readers of poetry. In his essay "Donne in Our Time," Eliot develops the thesis that a poet in the early part of his career should find a particular poet or a particular school of poetry for whom or for which he feels a close sympathy and because of whom he can train his talent. To a large degree, Baudelaire was that poet for Eliot.

In his last essay on Baudelaire, that of 1930, Eliot repeated the thought of his important sentence: "Man is man because he can recognize supernatural realities, not because he can invent them." Villon's poetry, as well as Baudelaire's, was for Eliot an unconsciously Christian poetry. In answer to an interview in *La France Libre* in 1944 (15 June), Eliot, in explaining what France meant to him, said that if he had not discovered Baudelaire, and the lineage of Baudelairian poets, he believed he would not have become a writer.

The new American poetry, which derived from neither the tradition of Poe, emphasizing subjectivism and musical qualities, nor the tradition of Whitman, more rhetorical and popular, was born in London about 1915. The influence of the French symbolists marked and enriched all of the new poetry. W. B. Yeats, in Chicago, on the evening of 1 March 1914, in the rooms of the Cliff Dwellers, where he was being honored at a dinner given by *Poetry* magazine, said in a speech reported in the April 1914 issue: "It is from Paris that nearly all the great influences in art and literature have come, from the time of Chaucer until now." Yeats spoke bluntly about "the sentimentality, the rhetoric, the moral uplift" he found in American periodicals, and claimed that those traits existed not because Americans were too far from England, but because they were too far from Paris. He related an incident in Paris when he met Paul Verlaine. He asked Verlaine why the French poet did not translate Tennyson, and Verlaine replied to Yeats that Tennyson was "too Anglais, too noble" to be translated into French. Yeats added to his praise of French literature his belief that "the best English writing is dominated by French criticism; in France is the great critical mind."

In 1910 Eliot lived in Paris, where he took courses at the Sorbonne and private French lessons from Alain-Fournier, who was to publish *Le Grand Meaulnes* in 1913. The Paris that Eliot observed in 1910 was the past and future of the city: *Les Cahiers de la Quinzaine* were appearing at that time in Péguy's shop; enthusiasm for Henri Bergson filled an auditorium in the Collège de France to capacity every week; *La Nouvelle Revue Française* was really *new*. Many years later, in speaking of the year 1910 in an article of homage to Jacques

Rivière, Eliot said that for him at that time "France represented poetry." There he was attracted to the work of Laforgue, Corbière, Verlaine, Baudelaire, Rimbaud, and Gautier. He was also reading certain French prose writers: Stendhal, Flaubert, the Goncourt brothers, Benda, and Jacques Maritain.

Of all these French writers, Baudelaire had the deepest influence on Eliot. With Baudelaire, he felt the closest affinities: affinities even in temperament and reserve of character, in the challenge of self-discipline and the pursuit of a difficult art, and in the desire to create a different art. Baudelairian dandyism, visible in Eliot's personality and appearance, was first an isolation, but it was especially the heroism of concentration, the spiritual struggle for inner perfection.

Almost at the same time in their careers, when they were still quite young, Baudelaire and Eliot realized that the poet and the critic are one. Both poets felt the reciprocal dependence of their critical and creative faculties.

Baudelaire taught Eliot ways by which to renew the poetic art by drawing from the daily life of a large metropolis. He taught the American poet especially the way to translate ideas into sensations. "Prufrock," as a love song, is reminiscent of Laforgue's *Complaintes*, or even of Apollinaire's *La Chanson du mal-aimé*.

Bergson used to say that poets understand and feel the concept of time better than philosophers. This preoccupation with time, common to Baudelaire and Eliot, points out more lucidly than other preoccupations the close bonds existing between the poetic work and the spirituality of the writers. The nostalgic resurrection of the past, apparent throughout all of Eliot's work, but especially in *Four Quartets*, is related to Baudelaire's *Correspondances*:

> *Comme de longs échos qui de loin se confondent*
> *Dans une ténébreuse et profonde unité.*

> (Like long echoes that from a distance are mingled
> In a dark and profound unity.)

More fervently than any other poet of the twentieth century, Eliot has sung of the permanence of time, the experience of one time that is all time. He sings of it when he speaks of the flowers that wilt, of the sea that seems eternal, of the rock in the sea, and of the prayer of the Annunciation.

There is no end of it, the voiceless wailing,
No end to the withering of withered flowers,
To the movement of pain that is painless and motionless,
To the drift of the sea and the drifting wreckage,
The bone's prayer to Death its God. Only the hardly,
   barely prayable
Prayer of the one Annunciation.

("The Dry Salvages," II)

In such a passage, as in the best passages of Baudelaire (*La servante au grand coeur*), the poet reveals his true mission, that of transmuting his intimate emotions, his personal anguish, into a strange and impersonal work. Thus the poet becomes aware of his presence in the world, where his major victory is the imposing of his presence as a man by means of his lucidity and his creative power.

4

Stéphane Mallarmé:
The Poet and the Clown

Stéphane Mallarmé enunciated in many ways and on many occasions the belief that poetry is something akin to magic. After passing through the two phases of individualistic and social poetry with the early romantics and Victor Hugo, it became, especially with Mallarmé, a metaphysical exercise. He married the arts without hesitation, one with the other. His defense of the new painting in his day was undertaken with as much fervor as was his defense of the new poetry and new drama.

Recent critics and biographers of Mallarmé have tried to discover the philosophical books and authors that might have served as the foundation of his aesthetics. But Mallarmé was probably not an assiduous reader of the German metaphysicians, even of Fichte and Hegel, with whom his name has been associated. He doubtless read very little technical philosophy, and had no characteristics of the erudite, which Flaubert, for example, possessed. He was of course aware of the philosophical concepts in his day, but his mind deepened by means of perceptions rather than dialectics. Pascal would have called Mallarmé *un esprit de finesse* (spirit of subtlety). The series of seemingly unrelated or discontinuous images that many of his poems demonstrate place them beside the work of the post-impressionists, cubists, and surrealists.

Unlike those writers for whom writing was a constant career—Voltaire or Victor Hugo—Mallarmé was one of those poets like Baudelaire and Valéry, whose far rarer productions were the result of certain privileged moments in a lifetime. As with the painters who were his friends—Manet, Degas, Berthe Morisot—and with the great painters who followed him, Mallarmé had only a few subjects in his poems. Like a portrait painter, he waited for commissions. His poems were of circumstances or occasions.

In the early years, what seemed to him poetic sterility, or lack of material, was the cause of personal anxiety. It became one of the principles of his aesthetic beliefs. The poet's struggle with the white page is comparable to the painter's struggle with the white canvas. The infrequent sonnets of Mallarmé and the still-lifes of Braque, for example, represent a difficult attitude toward nature and the familiar objects of a room. The newer artist, both poet and painter, is more isolated from the world in his almost obsessive treatment of a few familiar objects, figures, and scenes. The often recurring treatment of the same objects in the sonnets of Mallarmé and in the paintings of Picasso lent itself to the art of deforming the presences and the objects.

Symbolism and impressionism both were reactions to the data, the given subject material, the rigor in order and composition of an Ingres or a Leconte de Lisle. The so-called cult of obscurity, as opposed to an oratorical or expository art, is certainly to some degree the art of doubt and nuance, an art based on a predilection for ellipsis. Mallarmé, in the very title of his collected essays, *Divagations*, warns that he will turn the reader's mind from the usual ways and channels. He was fully aware that his poetry was an arduous exercise for the mind and a delicate testing of the sensibility.

Mallarmé's habit of living in his apartment more than in the world parallels his withdrawal from popular literature and his creation of a highly esoteric poetry. The fan, vases, books, and bibelots of his parlor helped to constitute the scene of a refuge not unlike *la chambre bleue* of Mme. de Rambouillet, in which manners and the art of poetry were protected from the coarseness of the court of Henri IV. Beyond any doubt, Mallarmé believed that the highest or the purest expressions of art were accessible to very few.

Words have familiar meanings, and this fact represented for the poet the constant trap or obstacle to the creation of his kind of poem. Likewise, the objects painted by Braque and Matisse were to suggest rather than signify. Mallarmé turned more and more to the negative word, the word of absence, as in his toast sonnet, *Salut,*

Rien, cette écume, vierge vers

(Nothing, this foam, virginal verse)

and the use of a series of seemingly disjointed or discontinuous images, as in the sonnet on Baudelaire's tomb. The successive images, flaming and fulgurant, in *La chevelure vol d'une flamme* ("The Hair Flight of a Flame"), prevent a solemn exercise of relationships that have to be seized by the reader. Such demands on the reader are not unlike the demands of a spectator, implied in such a painting as Picasso's *Les demoiselles d'Avignon.*

The difficult and often painful existence of the poet and artist we associate with Baudelaire, Mallarmé, Cézanne, or Van Gogh, with their failures, exile, and sadness, seems a necessary part of the scheme whereby they will see the purer, more spiritual vision of things and their relationships. Proust has spoken in detail about the disparity between the artist's life and his work. Alfred de Vigny's ivory tower is the symbol of the poet's isolation and dignity. Mallarmé's salon and Verlaine's café were in one sense their ivory towers.

In the history of French poetry, Mallarmé represents today a turning point and a point of achievement. His art and theory are of such a nature that his moment has the significance of the *trobar clus* (hermetic style) of the troubadours of the twelfth century, of the Platonists of the Renaissance, and of romanticism and the Parnassian ideal, which immediately preceded him in the nineteenth century. By his concentration on language, by his skill with ellipsis and synecdoche, Mallarmé purified language. Only the more efficacious words remained in the finished line to designate the object and the way in which it was seen. This purification of language was such that the object revealed was elevated to a metaphysical value: the swan, the punished clown, the helmet of the girl empress—each reaches meanings far beyond the usual.

A poem is a privileged moment when words are revealed in a new context, in an unusual light, an unusual drama: the sun-flooded noon of the faun in the forest, or the cold midnight of Hérodiade in her tower. But whatever the object—a lascivious faun, a hieratic princess, a garden of irises, an empty bibelot—the theme of the poem is always the same: the poetic act.

In a letter to Verlaine in 1885, an important text called *Autobiographie*, Mallarmé names the ideal book he hopes to write: *Le livre, explication orphique de la Terre* (The Book, Orphic Explanation of the Earth). Metaphors are in reality metamorphoses and transmutations, and thus the poet, creator of metaphors, is a kind of alchemist and magician. The attempt to re-create the world by means of the poetic word is a quasi-divine ambition.

Mallarmé was fully conscious of the immemorial prestige of words: the meaning they have today in their human context, and the more esoteric meanings that still cling to them from their uses in a remote past. The moral theme, so strong in *Les Fleurs du Mal*, diminishes in Mallarmé's poems. The theory of verbal incantation, defined by Baudelaire, is more fully applied by Mallarmé, until the power of the words, with their associations and relationships, replaces the moral allusions. This would be a major distinction between Baudelaire's *Le Voyage*, in which the various kinds of voyage are moral quests, and Mallarmé's *Prose pour des Esseintes*, in which the island voyage is the poet's quest for beauty. The reality of Paris in *Le Cygne* is the basis of Baudelaire's art, whereas the real world is nullified in *Toast Funèbre* as Mallarmé celebrates the poetic universe created by the poet.

The experience of sterility, evident in *L'Azur*, followed the experience of purity. *Hérodiade* is perhaps the work that best designates this very marked change in Mallarmé's poetic process. What had once been for the romantics and even for Verlaine's poetry of the ephemeral became for Mallarmé an experience cast in the form of a drama—a drama of the mind in search of the absolute.

The poems of Mallarmé and his teaching about poetry mark a change in poetry's history of an art form. Poetry before him, on the whole, translated sentiments and ideas, and usually without ambiguity. Poetry after him is more difficult because it conforms to other powers of language, because it is the expression of mysterious aspects of existence. The charm and the processes of Mallarmé are visible in such different and original poets as Apollinaire, Valéry, Claudel, and Eluard. Mallarmé created an art form that is antioratorical and antisocial. By writing a poetry in which the concrete is always vanishing, he created a countercreation. The flower he holds up in his verse is not a flower—it is the one absent from all bouquets, *l'absente de tous bouquets*.

Le Pitre châtié
("The Punished Clown")

For more than twenty years, through a process of ellipsis, of whittling down the early Tournon verse of 1864, Mallarmé labored over and finally produced the definitive version of his sonnet on the clown, *le pitre châtié*. It is one of his most spectacular pieces, easily rivaling today his most frequently anthologized sonnet on the swan.

Le pitre châtié is about the clown's revolt against his vocation, about the poet's revolt against his calling. Clown and poet are inextricably bound together in this poem, where *le pitre* is Hamlet and Hamlet is *le pitre*.

It is a strongly hyperbolic poem, as all of Mallarmé's best poems are. And it is a travesty—the poet as *saltimbanque*. It is an autoportrait also: the clown-poet, as once Alfred Jarry assimilated the traits and language of his creature Ubu; as once Georges Rouault painted himself as the head of a tragic clown. These artists, and many others, appropriated for a sonnet, a play, and a painting the hero of the most popular of all the arts: the circus clown. Strange that the poet, the most secretive, the most personal, of all heroes is able to pass into the characterization of the clown, as Virgil once passed into the shepherds who sang in his verse.

But why not? The acrobat performing is the perfect allegory of the poet in the practice of his art. One is attached to his tent as the other is attached to the white paper. The exoticism of the fair or the circus for a child bears an analogy with the fame of the published poet who is known by many readers and whose poems create in their visions of beauty rich experiences of transport. The effects of the circus on a child—its noise, the skills it demonstrates, the hilarity it provokes—are magical effects. All of this has suddenly become quiet in Mallarmé's sonnet as we watch the drama of the clown leaving his tent.

This sonnet of an apostasy begins with two words, two syllables, *yeux, lacs*, the second in apposition to the first and together forming a powerful synecdoche. The "eyes" attract him, either the eyes of someone he loves or the eyes of the public, and he names them, by analogy, "lakes." After these two long syllables, *yeux, lacs*, which immediately set the theme and tone of the poem, it is wise to move to the action line of the quatrain, the fourth:

J'ai troué dans le mur de toile une fenêtre

(I cut an opening in the canvas wall)

It is the only direct line of the stanza. Deliberately, vigorously (*j'ai troué*), the clown makes a hole in the canvas (*toile*) and escapes. He describes the feeling this gives him if we return to the first line, which depends, after its first two words, on the action of line 4:

avec ma simple ivresse de renaître

(with my simple ecstasy to be reborn)

He has willed the escape, willed to turn renegade and begin life over in some other vocation. Lines 2 and 3 complete the quatrain:

Autre que l'histrion qui du geste évoquais
Comme plume la suie ignoble des quinquets.

(Other than the actor who evoked by gesture
As the pen evokes the base soot of the lamps.)

The new intoxication (*ivresse*) is not that of the clown. He is reborn, but not as the performer. The word *histrion* is analyzed in language typical of Mallarmé's congealed speech, and with a subtle grammatical twist that both conceals and explains the thought of the sonnet:

histrion qui du geste évoquais

The subject of *évoquais* is *histrion*, but it is in the first-person singular, and so we would have to read the line as *histrion, moi qui évoquais*: "the clown, I who evoked." This carries into the third line, the hardest line of the poem to explain.

It is a pun, a play on words that underscores the analogy between the actor and the poet. The line begins with *plume,* and one thinks first of the poet's pen, and then, because of an allusion soon to come in the poem, of a Hamlet-like cap with a feather in it—a costume symbol of the supreme theater hero, Hamlet. The line ends with *quinquets,* and again two settings are evoked: the footlights, or the lamps placed along the edge of the stage, and the poet's lamp, lighted for so long during a night's vigil that it becomes covered with filthy soot (*suie ignoble*). Gestures of the actor have to be rehearsed over and over, and he has to play before a public again and again before he achieves a satisfactory performance. The poet writes and rewrites his lines under a smoky lamp.

Is the poet, then, the clown of the Muse? From the earliest version of the sonnet, Mallarmé condenses the first two lines into two words with which the definitive version begins—*Yeux, lacs*—and establishes by this juxtaposition an alliance, a correspondence between "eyes" and "lakes," into which plunge a lover and a swimmer. The plunge is an experience of exaltation (*ivresse*). It is a willful act of separation from the familiar: from the closed-in room with the lamp (if the protagonist is poet-lover) or from the closed-in tent (if the protagonist is clown-lover). The swimmer is the new man, the man liberated from his condition of clown tyrannized by his compulsion to perform and from his condition of poet tyrannized by his compulsion to write.

The sonnet's second quatrain is the picture of the lake, the site of betrayal, and the new kind of performance of the clown-poet now turned swimmer (*nageur*). The movement of the swimmer in the water would seem to be a continuation of clowning:

> *De ma jambe et des bras limpide nageur traître*
> *A bonds multipliés . . .*

(With my leg and arms limpid treacherous swimmer
in successive leaps . . .)

He propels himself through the waters like a frog, by jerky movements, his legs close together as if they were one leg. The new element through which he propels himself reveals him naked (*limpide*), stripped of his clown's costume, and therefore a traitor (*traître*) to his tent, through which he had ripped a hole for his escape. Whatever his original site was, a circus booth or the temple of the Muse, he has deserted it, and the verb he uses to designate the change is a strong one:

> *. . . reniant le mauvais*
> *Hamlet! c'est comme si dans l'onde j'innovais*
> *Mille sépulcres pour y vierge disparaître.*

(denying the bad
(Hamlet! it is as if in the water I innovated
A thousand sepulchres to disappear there a virgin.)

The "bad Hamlet" is the *histrion* of the first quatrain, and this specifically named hero reiterates and justifies all the complexities of the drama with which Mallarmé is here concerned.

Hamlet the doubter, hesitating to undertake any action, was, after all, the hero par excellence, and the poet as well. The word *histrion* never had for Mallarmé a pejorative meaning. The histrionic clown, in rejecting the ineffectual ham actor in himself, still remains the comic by his jerky movements in the lake. Each time his head disappears under the surface, it is as if he were entering his tomb and making himself new and virginal as he dives from sight.

The lake, a pure metaphor at the beginning of the sonnet, is now the experience itself of escape and renewal. The clown has defied the interdiction to leave the site of his performances. Hamlet has suddenly, in the midst of a performance, left the stage, where nightly he recites the lines of the poet. The protagonist of the sonnet has abandoned that artificial place associated with his vocation.

The two tercets are closely joined. Together they form one sentence. Swimming in the lake, the hero is struck by the sun in his new vulnerability of nakedness. The blow is so strong that it is transcribed as the clashing of cymbals:

Hilare or de cymbale à des poings irrité,
Tout à coup le soleil frappe la nudité
Qui pure s'exhala de ma fraîcheur de nacre, . . .

(Like joyous gold of cymbals attached to wrists
Suddenly the sun, irritated, strikes the nudity
That is exhaled pure from the coolness of my white body, . . .)

In this long sentence of the two tercets (lines 9–14), the golden cymbals are in apposition to the sun, and the word *irrité* applies to the sun, representing the source of the punishment. The use of cymbals, a psalmlike religious word, evokes a rite that is unfolding. But it is also a circus sound announcing a new "number." The brass disks of the cymbal, held aloft in the hands of a musician, resemble the sun in the sky. The body of the swimmer, washed by the water, is like mother-of-pearl (*nacre*) and is openly vulnerable to the sun's rays, instruments of punishment striking the man who has betrayed his trust and his vocation.

The second tercet continues the scene of punishment with a word in strong opposition to the sun:

Rance nuit de la peau quand sur moi vous passiez
Ne sachant pas, ingrat! que c'etait tout mon sacre,
Ce fard noyé dans l'eau perfide des glaciers.

(Rancid night of the skin when you passed over me
Not knowing, ungrateful one, that my only consecration was
This makeup paint drowned in the perfidious water of glaciers.)

The entire first line of this last stanza is explained by the third line.
Rance nuit de la peau is the greasepaint of the clown, or possibly the
dark costume of Hamlet, and it stands in apposition to *ce fard*, the
"rouge" or "makeup" that has been washed away by the action of the
water—the icy water of glaciers that feed the lake. The *vous*, in "where
you passed over me," would seem to be the plural word *glaciers*, a
central word in Mallarmé's vocabulary because it is a word of absence
and purity, a pivotal word ending the sonnet and relating back to
the opening word, *yeux*. The "eyes" were the mirage of the clown's
temptation, and the "glaciers" are the cold, hard reality of punishment.

Behind the word *ivresse* of the first line, announcing the exaltation
of escape and freedom, one can easily sense the *angoisse* of the prisoner, who has made up his mind to leap into the unknown. Clown
or Hamlet or poet, he is sickened by his nightly performances, his
exercises endlessly repeated, rehearsed, rewritten, and he longs to
know the pure elements of another world that is not closed in by walls
and lighted by lamps, airless, where the public, real or imaginary,
stares at him, as they wait to be amazed or moved. He appears before
them, disguised by makeup or by the words he recites.

But once in the waters of his new freedom, he begins the harass-
ing experience of disillusionment. He is not the swimmer or the
lover or the liberated man he had dreamed of becoming. His jerky
movements propelling him through the water are clownish too,
repeated over and over, in an element that freezes him, and where,
without costume and makeup, he feels the chastisement of heaven:
a flash of sunlight or lightning that reminds him of a resounding
stage entrance. Such a shock was necessary for him to realize the
seriousness of his mistake. Liberated? Yes, but his actions are now
a countless series of descents into a tomb.

The clown had once been that man, personified for Mallarmé in
Hamlet, caught and cloistered in one place for a given length of
time, a human conscience unable to act, unable to become. So the
subject of *Le pitre châtié* is a man's revolt against his vocation. It is

a poem on apostasy, or, in terms of a more positive note, a need for rebirth. The name "Hamlet" is synonymous with theater, and Shakespeare himself has said that the theater is the microcosm of life, where each man plays a part. The stage, then, is that place where each of us has to live. But we have learned that the stage, as the focal part of the theater, is the source of metamorphoses where a public can watch the dramatic contrast between what a man is and what he wants to be.

Mallarmé indicates a subtle analogy between the sheet of paper on which the poet writes, the white canvas that the painter transforms, and the backdrop against which the actor performs. The paper, the canvas, and the backdrop are real material objects for the artist, but are charged with such obsessiveness and power that we are inclined to call them objects possessing a mystical force that separates the poet, the painter, and the clown-actor from the real world.

The makeup of the actor, *ce fard*, is the consecration of the genius, and so acknowledged by the clown at the end of the poem. The performer's makeup is that which permits the public to see him, as the words of the poet, the sign of his genius, permit us to read and feel the projection of an idea.

An idea has to be made theatrical in order to live. A man has to be metamorphosed into a clown in order to be seen and believed and understood. On a page of paper, on a stage, and on a sheet of canvas, a collision may take place between art and life.

Eliot—Poe—Mallarmé

The strong influence of Poe on three major French poets of three generations still remains something of an enigma. Baudelaire, Mallarmé, and Valéry felt his influence in varying ways. Throughout almost a century this fascination for Edgar Allan Poe continued. The most sensitive assessment of this curious chapter in the history of modern poetics has been made by Eliot in his essay written in French.

No literary reputation has ever been established once and for all. English and American critics tend to see in the works of Poe defects and limitations. But three French poets of major importance have studied Poe and discovered in him traits and illuminations that his native American critics have not discussed. No American or English poet has ever claimed Poe to be his master. Looked upon as a minor "romantic" poet, Poe is usually classified as a successor to writers of "Gothic tales." During the past half a century, when interest in Walt Whitman and praise for his work have increased, Poe has been neglected and even forgotten.

The rhythm and incantatory effect of Poe's poetry still delights young readers. Others, slightly older, enjoy the stories. Still older readers look upon him as the forerunner of Sir Arthur Conan Doyle, creator of Sherlock Holmes. In discussing the immediate, an almost magical effect of the sound of Poe's lines, Eliot draws a clear distinction between "verse," with which he qualifies Poe's art of versification, and "poetry," by which he defines the classical versification of Shakespeare and Milton. Often Poe uses a word for its tonal quality and sound when it does not have an exact meaning in the context of the line.

In contradicting Poe's famous theory concerning the impossibility of a long poem (as a text unable to sustain one concentrated effect), Eliot points out that Poe was probably incapable of writing a long poem. Poe claimed that a poem should have one simple effect. Eliot claimed that a long poem has a succession or variety of effects. This theory could be easily illustrated in *Four Quartets*.

Baudelaire was fascinated by the story of Poe's life, by what he believed to be Poe's temperament, by the type of poet beset by "bad luck," by *le guignon*. Poe was the prototype of what Verlaine, later in the century, will call *le poète maudit*, "the poet under a curse." Baudelaire admired Poe as being that type of poet—worshipper of beauty and perfection, who, at the same time, is the victim of that worship.

This image of the poet as lover of beauty contains the germ of an aesthetic that lasted for a century in France and in countries that followed the aesthetics of symbolism. "Pure poetry" (*la poésie pure*) is this far-reaching doctrine. In speaking of Poe, Baudelaire wrote, "He believed that poetry should have no other matter in mind than itself" (*Il croyait que la poésie ne doit pas avoir en vue autre chose qu'elle-même*). The subject of a poem therefore remains important, but as a means only. The goal of the poem is the poem itself.

The poet is primarily the craftsman who organizes words into structures. Poe's statement that "a poem has an architecture" was attractive to Baudelaire and other symbolists. Baudelaire read Poe in 1846–47, and took over the doctrine that poetry has to do with the beautiful. Poetry is not the result of inspiration but the reward of daily effort.

In "The Poetic Principle," Poe's essay-lecture of 1850, he emphasized all these thoughts and converted them into a poetics, into a poetic manifesto. He denounced the heresy of the didactic, that is, the use of a poem for underscoring a moral or religious issue, or for revealing a bit of knowledge. Poetry is, Poe insists in his strongest phrase, "the rhythmical creation of beauty." Poetry's sole arbiter is taste.

Baudelaire, in translating the stories of Poe, and Mallarmé, in translating the poems, improved the texts of the American writer. After them, Paul Valéry, in his admiration for *Eureka*, carried far the interpenetration of Poe's poetic and critical activity. The influence of Poe on French poets, so judiciously studied by Eliot, points out the historical fact that such influence may be very different, even foreign, from a native American's appreciation of Poe.

Le Tombeau d'Edgar Poe

Mallarmé, like other Frenchmen attracted to Poe, thought of him as a tragic, isolated genius who had unusual critical powers, a man unappreciated in America. Mallarmé wrote his name as *Poë*, and from there to making him a representative *poet* was an obvious step. In line 2 of his sonnet, he calls him *Le Poëte*, with a capital letter, and names him in line 11, *la tombe de Poe*.

Poe was so forgotten after his death (1849) that his grave in Baltimore was without a tombstone for twenty years. Then between 1875 and 1877 plans were made and carried out to place a stone on his grave and mark it with a ceremony and the publishing of a book of homage. According to W. H. Auden, the only American author to attend the ceremony was Walt Whitman. In the "Memorial Volume" (1877), one can find *Le Tombeau d'Edgar Poe* and Mallarmé's own translation of it into English. Mallarmé had never forgotten how Baudelaire, in his *Journaux intimes*, named in his daily prayers Poe as intercessor with God.

All the themes coalesce here: the poet, poetry, the public, time. All the figures too: angel, hydra, Oedipus, sphinx. And finally the three names central to our inquiry: Poe, Mallarmé, and Eliot.

> *Tel qu'en Lui-même enfin l'éternité le change,*
> *Le Poëte suscite avec un glaive nu*
> *Son siècle épouvanté de n'avoir pas connu*
> *Que la mort triomphait dans cette voix étrange.*

> (Such as into Himself at last eternity changes him,
> The Poet resurrects with a bare sword
> His century terrified at not having known
> That death triumphed in that strange voice.)

The opening line states in its twelve syllables the message of this sonnet. The poet disappears behind his poem. The words he wrote are what remains of him: the purified form of his being. Both Hegel and Sartre, in their own formulas, have expressed this thought that a man can be identified, "finally," only after his death.

The poet appears as a symbolic archangel holding a bare sword in his hand. This sword, the work of the poet, is his one weapon. The French phrase, *le glaive de la parole* ("the sword of the word"), stands for the power of speech, the power of eloquence. And the poet's century (*son siècle*) is his public frightened at not having recognized the power of his voice. The verb "triumph" is the echo-antithesis of "death." The poet's "strange voice" could easily be "the philosopher's or the scientist's strange voice."

Two words, one in the first quatrain and one in the title, bear an interesting relationship to *glaive* ("sword"). The pronoun in the first line, *Lui* (capitalized), recalls the verb *luire* ("to shine," the past participle of which is *lui*). The sword in the hand of an angel would appear to be shining. And Edgar, Poe's first name, is a compound of the Old English words *ead*, meaning "rich," or "happy," and *gar*, meaning "spear." The French poet sees in "Edgar" a "happy warrior with a spear."

Eux, comme un vil sursaut d'hydre oyant jadis l'ange
Donner un sens plus pur aux mots de la tribu,
Proclamèrent très haut le sortilège bu
Dans le flot sans honneur de quelque noir mélange.

(They, like a vile tremor of a hydra hearing long ago the angel
Give a purer meaning to the words of the tribe,
Proclaimed loudly the witchcraft drunk
From the honorless wave of some dark mixture.)

"They" (*eux*) refers back to Poe's century (*siècle*) and stands here in apposition to the monstrous figure of a hydra, a many-headed reptile. The "angel" (whose sword cuts off the heads of the hydra) speaks. He is the poet of the first quatrain, and his speech gives a purer meaning to the ordinary words spoken by everyone. The poet's language is so different from the usual language that it has to be deciphered.

For his pupils Mallarmé wrote a short treatise on mythology he called *Les Dieux Antiques*. Under the heading of "Oedipus" (*Oedipe*) he indicates an important clue to the first two lines of the second quatrain. The "hydra" is the "sphinx" and the poet is Oedipus. Thus the Oedipus story is translated into the sonnet on Poe. Every myth, Mallarmé declares in this note, is based on the combat of the angelic sun and the clouds that obscure it. The word "cloud" appears at the beginning of the first tercet:

> *Du sol et de la nue hostiles, ô grief!*
> *Si notre idée avec ne sculpte un bas-relief*
> *Dont la tombe de Poe éblouissante s'orne,*
>
> *Calme bloc ici-bas chu d'un désastre obscur,*
> *Que ce granit du moins montre à jamais sa borne*
> *Aux noirs vols du Blasphème épars dans le futur.*

(Hostile earth and clouds, O grievance!
If our idea does not sculpt a bas-relief
Decorating Poe's dazzling tomb

Calm block fallen down here from an obscure disaster
May this granite at least show forever its warning
To the dark flights of blasphemy scattered in the future.)

The earth and the sky (*sol et nue*) are the two poles of nature. In the tercets Mallarmé sees the tombstone as being a meteorite that has fallen from its star (disaster: dis-aster), and thus gives a cosmic quality to this fall. The granite meteor has reached the earth's surface without being vaporized. Thus it will constitute a limit (*borne*), a warning, placed on all blasphemies against the poet and his language by future posterity. The word *futur* in line 14 is synonymous with *éternité* in line 1. His death makes the poet invulnerable and uniquely poet.

   In "Little Gidding," the fourth of the *Quartets,* Eliot has translated word for word Mallarmé's line:

> *donner un sens plus pur aux mots de la tribu*

> To purify the dialect of the tribe

This passage begins, in an almost historical sense, with Eliot's early ruminations about poetic language, and, again, historically acknowledges his debt to the example and the art of the French poet:

Our concern was speech . . .

Mallarmé had seen young Rimbaud only once, at a gathering of poets in Paris, and in a few pages he wrote about him (some of which he sent in a letter to Rimbaud's mother after the poet's death), he calls him *un météore.*
As far as I know, Rimbaud made no mention of Mallarmé in his writing.

The difference between what Mallarmé represented to the world at the time of his death in 1898 and what he represents today, ninety years later, has the proportions of an almost miraculous change. It is an alteration that justifies and illuminates the opening line of the sonnet on Poe, who is finally changed into himself by eternity.
For the academic world in 1898, Stéphane Mallarmé was a teacher of English in the lycées of Paris who had asked in 1894 for an early retirement, to the relief of his officers and superiors. For the general public in Paris, interested in literature and art, Mallarmé was a dreamer, a dilettante, an aesthete (to use only the polite terms), who willfully obscured his infrequent publications in order to make them incomprehensible to any normally minded, normally constituted reader.
But fortunately there remained a third group, more restricted in numbers than the other two: the circle of devoted friends, most of whom were either poets or painters. Many of them attended the Tuesday evening gatherings in Mallarmé's apartment on the rue de Rome. A few of the painters—Manet, Whistler, Berthe Morisot—he called on regularly in their studios. These rare individuals found Mallarmé to be a loyal, warm friend, whose speech, whose conversation, was unsurpassed in brilliance, in a capital famed for the verbal wit and profundity of its inhabitants.
Those who were closest to him and who heard him from week to week knew that he was a kind of contemplative who meditated and actually thought before speaking. One after another, those belonging to the older group of friends (Dujardin, Fontainas, Mockel) and the younger disciples (Gide, Valéry, Gauguin, Vuillard) acknowledged that Mallarmé and his sympathetic devotion had helped to teach them who they were. After the creation of his own work, Mallarmé's greatest role was the revealer of genius. If he was not an able pedagogue in the classroom, he was a gentle, attentive pedagogue for some of the most gifted poets and painters of the late nineteenth century.

When, in the second decade of this century, Albert Thibaudet requested permission to present a thesis on Mallarmé at the Sorbonne, he was turned down as if he had perpetrated a bad joke. Independently of the Sorbonne, he published his study—a true pioneer work—in 1925. Since that time, during the past sixty years, theses, books, and articles on Mallarmé have multiplied. There is today a vast literature concerned with an effort to interpret his poetry. His work is seen to represent the final stage and the most dazzling achievement in a veritable revolution concerning the craft and meaning of poetry. According to Mallarmé, poetry is a talisman that may open up the way to a metaphysical life in man. He would not have reached this belief without the examples before him of Hugo, Baudelaire, Nerval, and Rimbaud.

Once the symbolist poet André Fontainas approached Mallarmé at a gathering and spoke to him about a magnificent tree in a painting of Claude Monet that he had just seen exhibited in the window of a gallery. Mallarmé concurred in enthusiasm over the new painting of the tree, and said: "Yes, it's a superb Monet, a peacock burning the landscape with its spread-out tail" (*Le Monet superbe, un paon brûlant le paysage de sa queue étalée*).

This analogy was startling, in the good Mallarmé tradition, but a bystander, overhearing it, chided the poet. "Come now, Mallarmé," he said, "is the picture a peacock or is it a tree?" The art of Claude Monet had a very special appeal for Mallarmé. It was personal, like Mallarmé's own art, very willful, fragmentary, fleeting, with its ecstatic play of light on fields, stones, water. Once, in speaking with Berthe Morisot, Mallarmé said he was happy to live in the same period in history as Monet: "*Je suis heureux de vivre à la même époque que Monet.*"

The object exists in an impressionist painting and in a Mallarmé sonnet, but it does not exist for and by itself. It creates, in the art of painting, a luminous concept, an "impression" coming from the object and reducing the object's importance in the fleeting lights and shadows it is composed of. This hope of painting the very instability of matter and of capturing a single moment in its varied tonalities of light was far too ambitious in its absolute sense. And likewise, the goal of Mallarmé, to discover and write the Orphic meaning of the world, was destined to failure. Painters and poets alike embarked upon a veritable renovation of technique.

Soon after the turn of the century, Mallarmé's influence was felt on the new poetry, about the time when Cézanne began influencing the new painters. These two artists who hardly knew one another exerted telling influences on modern art. Cubism, in particular, owed a great deal to the plastic forms in Cézanne's paintings, and the importance Mallarmé paid to signs or symbols in his poems encouraged a comparable boldness in the cubist painters.

The central lesson in Mallarmé's aesthetic concerns the incantatory power of words. In a two-page essay, *"Magie,"* he points out that the medieval study of alchemy, when it disappeared with the Middle Ages, left in its wake, for the modern mind, two studies: aesthetics, on the one hand, and economics, on the other (*économie politique*). He claimed that alchemy was "the glorious and mysterious forerunner of economics." The philosophers' stone, referred to so often in the Middle Ages, whose function was to produce gold, announced, according to Mallarmé, in the new world of finance what is called "credit" and what precedes "capital," or what reduces it to the humble state of mere money!

Between poetry and witchcraft there has always existed a secret equivalence. What the poet does is close to a mystical creation. By means of words that are allusive and not direct, he calls up an object that had been silenced. The words begin to glow and mean until the illusion they evoke is equivalent to what the eyes of a man can see in the material world. *Le vers, trait incantatoire* (the verse, an act of incantation).

The language the poet creates is a bond between himself, his own consciousness, and the consciousness of the world around him. The uncertainty of human action is made into the firm, fixed language of metaphor, and there the poet welcomes and strengthens all the hesitancies, all the uncertainties, all the torments, of human experience. When the poem is achieved, that which is most impersonal in a poet enters into a strange impersonal work. T. S. Eliot, in his early essay, "Tradition and the Individual Talent," gives firm expression to this belief. The major poems of Mallarmé are brilliant testimonials to Eliot's theory.

The drama of poetic creation is bare in Baudelaire, but in Mallarmé it is projected into the forest scene of the nymphs where the faun, playing his pipes, wonders whether he can perpetuate his desire with music or satisfy his desire by separating the nymphs one from the other. In *Bénédiction*, Baudelaire adumbrates the poet's drama almost in the form of biography, whereas in *L'Après-Midi d'un faune*, it is recast into the age-old myth of the soul eager to know itself. Mallarmé is not a metaphysician in any literal sense, but he is a poet haunted by metaphysics.

The ambition to reach the absolute is a predestined failure. The irises (*iridées*, both *iris* and *idées*) multiply and grow to such an extent that the will of the poet in his island adventure of *Prose pour des Esseintes* is frustrated. The warm hour of noon for the faun-musician is in reality an hour of sterility when he sings of passion rather than experiencing passion. The counterpoint of words, of Mallarmé's words, is the final trap, the final capitulation, where action is held in a steadfast grip, and the cry of passion is modulated into a single clear melodic line. The darkness and the silence of evening are always just beyond the poem's last line. They are waiting for the last line to be said. They are waiting to take over.

But Mallarmé translated into poems a human experience and not a system of metaphysics. He understood the implications of the poetic doctrine as defined by Baudelaire and Poe, of poetry being the object of beauty, of a poem being looked upon as the search for an effect. Such a poetic doctrine, however important it is, would not fully account for the great poems of Mallarmé. The personal crisis of 1866, which seems to have been largely of a psychological nature, plays a vital role in the creation of the future poems. The discovery of such a concept as the void (*le néant*) is as important as Mallarmé's decision to avoid in his poems mere analyses of impressions and depictions of sentiments.

To the experience of sterility, evident in such a poem as *L'Azur*, succeeded the experience of absence or of purity. *Hérodiade* indicates this marked change in Mallarmé's poetic process. The beauty of the world and its absence are fused into the subject matter of his poems. The poem is the dream, at once real and unreal. To recall a dream is to blow it up, as the faun blows into the empty skin of the grapes after he has sucked out the juice. The notes of his flute are the drops of cool water falling over the forest scene. The music played by the faun in the forest sustains his dream, which had vanished, and the poem sustains and prolongs the poet's dream, which also had vanished. A poem is inevitably for Mallarmé a poem about absence.

Visions spring from words. A poem is a human invention. When it is read sympathetically, it begins the extraordinary adventure of re-creating itself and of creating what is beyond itself. The object-symbol is merely an investiture, and something real emerges from it which is the real poem.

5

Arthur Rimbaud:
Mémoire

Rimbaud began writing at an early age in Charleville, in the Ardennes in northern France. In 1869 a Latin poem he wrote won first prize in the Concours Académique. His first known French poem, *Les Etrennes des Orphelins* ("The Orphans' Gifts"), was composed in the same year, when he was fifteen.

During 1870 he wrote twenty-two poems. The young teacher Georges Izambard became Rimbaud's mentor and friend during his last year at the Collège de Charleville. On 29 August, Rimbaud made his first escape to Paris, by train, and was put into Mazas prison at the end of the trip because he had not purchased a full ticket. Later, in October, he set out for Belgium, an experience that inspired such poems as *Ma Bohème, Le Buffet*, and *Au Cabaret Vert* ("My Bohemian Life," "The Cupboard," and "The Cabaret Vert").

There was another trip to Paris, in February 1871, and a return on foot to Charleville. His two letters of May to Izambard and Paul Demeny are in reality treatises on Rimbaud's conception of poetry. The boy's disposition was strongly antireligious at this time, testified to in such a poem as *Les Premières Communions* ("First Communion"). At the end of September, Rimbaud, armed with new poems, including *Le Bateau Ivre* (The Drunken Boat), went to Paris, where he had been invited by Verlaine after a first exchange of letters.

The next two years were dominated by Verlaine in an enthusiastic, troubled, and at times tragic homosexual relationship. Rimbaud probably began writing some of the *Illuminations* in London in 1872, and was engaged in writing *Une Saison en Enfer* (A Season in Hell) in April 1873 at his mother's farm in Roche, near Charleville. The definitive break between the two poets occurred in Brussels in July 1873 as the result of a violent quarrel. Verlaine fired a revolver, wounding Rimbaud in the left wrist, and was arrested and sentenced by the Belgian police court to two years in prison. His arm in a sling, Rimbaud returned to Roche, where he completed *Une Saison en Enfer*. He was nineteen, and his literary work was over, save for some *Illuminations* he may have written during the next year and a half.

After extensive travel in Europe, Rimbaud went to Aden in 1880 to work for an export company. In 1887 he sold guns to King Menelik in Choa, and between 1888 and 1891 he worked for a coffee exporter in Harar. A tumor on his right knee caused him to return to Marseille in May 1891. His leg was amputated. After a brief return to Charleville to be with his mother and sister, he was again hospitalized in Marseille and died there at the age of thirty-seven.

Most of Rimbaud's work was written between the ages of sixteen and nineteen. After the Brussels drama, he published *Une Saison en Enfer*, but as soon as the work was printed and a few copies distributed, he lost all interest in it. *Les Illuminations* was published by Verlaine for the first time in 1886. The first edition of the poems came out in 1891.

Today most of the poems in verse present few difficulties to a reader trained in the reading of modern poetry, but *Une Saison en Enfer* is still a troublesome text. The psychic experience related in it is as much that of our age as it is of one adolescent poet. The prose poems of *Les Illuminations* are still difficult to fathom.

Etiemble's thesis, of gigantic proportions, *Le Mythe de Rimbaud*, appearing in 1952–53, denounced the critical method of turning Rimbaud into a mythical figure—angel or demon, Catholic or surrealist, *voyant* or *voyou* (visionary or scoundrel). The texts of Rimbaud today in the 1980s attract both semioticians and more traditional exegetes.

Our age is one of revolt, and Rimbaud has given, in his literary work and in the example of his life, one of the most vibrant expressions of this revolt. There was nothing unusual about his life, save that the major events, transpiring while he was a practicing poet, were swift: the interruption of formal study, the escape from his provincial life, his friendship with Verlaine, the discovery that very few people in Paris were interested in him or in his talent, the break with Verlaine, the writing of *Une Saison en Enfer*, and soon after that, the irrevocable giving up of poetry.

The strange masterpieces of Rimbaud, and of other artists and writers who followed him—Apollinaire, Joyce, Picasso, Chagall, and the composer Satie—show a proclivity toward enigma and infantile imagination. At sixteen or seventeen, when he composed *Mémoire*, Rimbaud speaks of a child but evokes the most austere dramas of man and woman. The character of woman is analyzed by the symbol of the river, as Anna Livia Plurabelle is analyzed in Joyce's *Finnegans Wake*. In *Le Bateau Ivre*, the poet, after all his hyperbolic adventures, has to return to the parapets of Europe, and in *Mémoire* he cannot cut the cables of his boat. The metamorphoses of the horizons we follow in *Le Bateau Ivre*—the liberation of the boat, going down the river, its marine adventures, its return to the parapets of Europe—are the metamorphoses of Rimbaud's character by which he forces his imagination to plunge into the unknown.

In his practice of poetry, which is neither exclusively sentiment nor music, Rimbaud laid the basis for a new opening out onto a supernatural and surreal world, an art that later will be associated with Paul Claudel and René Char. In the mind's search for that absolute, which began in modern poetry with Baudelaire and Nerval and continued in diverse ways with Rimbaud, Mallarmé, Claudel, and Apollinaire, poetry changed from an art of lyricism to one of inquiry and exasperation, to a search for values and metaphysical assurances. The basis is the charter as set forth in *Correspondances*: the visible world is the image of a secret universe. The alchemy Rimbaud alludes to is one term for an age-long quest for certainty, the survival of a tradition that parallels the history of mankind. Man has to learn how to work back from the visible to the invisible.

Mémoire: The Poet's Art

The title of *Mémoire* could be used for all art. What is remembered in *Mémoire*, and what is re-created from memory, are so perfectly fused in the verbal communication that one experience is confided to the page, that of the poem itself. All art has a starting point in reality. The Meuse is the starting point in *Mémoire*, which is another poem on the river, and therefore a companion piece to *Le Bateau Ivre*.

Mémoire is also another piece on the theme of flight. The scene of the poem is the prairie that separates Charleville from Mézières. Across the prairie flows the Meuse River, and perpendicular to it stretch out railroad tracks in the direction of Paris. According to Paterne Berrichon, brother-in-law of Rimbaud, who, after the poet's death, appointed himself official interpreter of the poems, *Mémoire* describes Rimbaud's final flight to Paris, on 29 August 1870. This interpretation was accepted by the critics Renéville and Ruchon. Marcel Coulon believes the poem describes the departure of Rimbaud's father in August 1864, when the daughters were six and four and the sons ten and nine. "Elle" in the poem would then be Mme. Rimbaud, the mother. Etiemble and Gauclère are more justified in indicating the falseness of adhering to any one biographical explanation for such a poem. *Mémoire* is a poem of sensations and very faintly recalled and remembered episodes. Each sensation evokes others, and the poem grows, as a river does, by accumulating all manner of reflections: lights and objects, some of them real and others formed by suggestions and juxtapositions.

The five sections of eight lines each are five rapidly sketched pictures of the prairie and the river. Each of these pictures is dominated by a character on whose identification any final interpretation of the work will depend.

1. The protagonist of the first section is named in the opening words: *L'eau claire* (clear water). The river water, as bitter as the salt tears of childhood, at first appears subordinated to the white flashing bodies of women bathing in it. As they play in the water and with their clothes on the bank, they resemble white angels. The picture Rimbaud paints is like a canvas of Cézanne where the bathers are no more important than the river or the sky or the green fields. The poet interrupts his image with a negative exclamation: *non!* It is the river, *Elle sombre* (she dark), which, with its black arms, dominates the scene and pulls down from the surrounding hills shadows for curtains. The river in its bed, like the persistent symbol of woman, expels all the real and fleshy women, as impermanent as the angels they resemble, and recaptures the center of the picture.

2. A series of words in the second section: *tend, meuble, couches, robes, foi conjugale* (extends, fills, beds, dresses, conjugal faith), all precede and prepare the naming of the new protagonist: *L'Epouse*. The spouse dominates this scene. It is noon: the moment when the sun warms the earth. And the water is symbolic of the change in

being when the woman receives her husband. The spouse is like the river reflecting perfectly the rose sphere of the sun. The stanza speaks of the roundness of woman's sex: the golden louis, the warm eyelid, the mirror, and finally the rose sphere, which might be the reflection of the sun on the water as well as the sun itself. (In its ordinary connotation, the sun would represent the phallic symbol of the male.) Woman, then, as spouse, is the second character in *Mémoire*, the waiting fidelity, round and warm in her flesh, a receptacle for man's power, as the Meuse is the mirror of the sun.

3. The third and center section of the poem is the most dramatic, and, as might be expected from Rimbaud, the protagonist here is the mother. It is the prairie scene where the mother, too erect, crushes the flowers as she walks, and where the children, too obedient in the grass, read their red-leather-bound prize books. The severity of the family is not lessened in the vast freedom of the fields. But suddenly one member, either a boy or a man, either son or husband, containing in himself the whiteness of a thousand angels—all that purity of the white bodies of bathing women and workmen in the fields—goes off beyond the mountain, beyond the scene of false freedom. The mother (or wife), black and cold as the river, rushes after the one escaping. It is a wordless scene, and all the more tragic for that. As in a dance, only the actions count, only the movement of rushing off, in order to escape or to retrieve. The woman is matriarch, black against the flowers and the grass of the prairie, black in her chase after the white angel, as the river is black against the body of the earth.

4. After the violent movement of the third part, the fourth reflects a nostalgic mood. The woman has been abandoned, but now she is not the mother. She is the mistress-lover, and all her memories are those of sensuality. She remembers the young arms that held her, April moonlight on her bed, the secret germination of August nights. Now she is alone to weep and to listen to the wind in the poplar trees and to watch the labors of an old boatman in his motionless boat. The last image is the most developed in the poem: it closes the fourth section and fills the fifth. The youthfulness of love suddenly becomes old age, and the picture of amorous excitement is replaced by a scene of weeping and solitude. The image of the solitary boatman is that of a man dragging the riverbed for sand, and this introduces the final tableau.

5. The poet speaks for the first time. This unexpected use of "I" adds a second character to the main character of an episode. In this fifth section, the protagonist seems to be the boat immobilized on

the water by its chain. The boy is in the boat and he is frustrated in each of his desires. His arms are too short and his boat is too firmly attached for him to pull from the water either flower that tempts him—the yellow flower or the blue flower. The roses of the water reeds were devoured a long time ago, and the boat's chain is buried in some obscure deep mud. The boy is defeated and the boat, from which he tries to retrieve some color of life and some living symbol of freedom, is immobilized. Under the boat flows the deep freedom of the "clear water," which is an eye that sees limitlessly. Thus the river, as in the first stanza, turns out to be the protagonist, and the boy is not trying to conquer the boat but to reach the river itself and plunge into the low recesses of the eye that is watching him.

Finally it becomes clear that the five characters of *Mémoire*—the water, the spouse, the mother, the mistress, and the river—are the same character, the same protagonist. Five scenes in which the poet tries to analyze five attempts to understand his relation with nature, which is woman and everything that is not he, everything that is outside of him.

First (*l'eau claire*) is beauty, tranquil and close to him, familiar in his childhood stories and in the landscapes of his childhood re-creation. This is the boy's contemplation of woman, where no desire destroys his love.

Second (*l'Epouse*) is the vision of the wife jealous of the male, who is so gifted with sight and desire and infidelity that she must possess him and hold within herself the reality of his man-being.

Third (*Madame*) is the whirlwind of maternal tyranny, dark as a storm gathering its power in one corner of the universe to rush after the white angel escaping. Whether it be son or husband, it is always the male escaping toward the lost innocence of his spirit, away from the flesh bondage of the female.

Fourth (the abandoned mistress: *qu'elle pleure à présent*) (let her weep now) is the quieted wind in the trees, which recalls moments of passion and ecstasy, the memory of young womanhood submitting herself to the act of love and then being abandoned, with the wound on her body, to the solitude of other nights.

Fifth (*cet oeil d'eau*) (this eye of water) is the flowing life of the river, or rather the deep and cool permanency of earth and of woman, with whom man seeks in vain to reach contentment and self-realization. It is the continuing principle of life that man is unable to seize or arrest or comprehend. It is the principle of woman that man, in his natural state, is unable to accept.

This *memory* is a poem of wonderment, primitive in its acceptance of fate and physical frustration, religious in its awareness of spiritual mysteries that tie up the drama of man at a terrifying distance from his physical body. Between the first and the last scenes, where man is seen bound to the secretiveness of his own principle, unfold scenes of frantic search and experiment and dynamism. In all of the scenes a confusion of two dramas takes place: Rimbaud's personal drama (his relationship with his mother) and the universal drama of man (his relationship with the universe).

In cinematographic procession and juxtaposition, all the characters of the poet's life are merged with one—into one eidolon of changing proportions but always of permanent and recognizable traits. The recapture of innocence is the last haunting spiritual quest of man. *Mémoire* is a sequence of scenes in a boy's remembrance of this quest where, repeatedly on the verge of escaping into the realm of freedom, and therefore of purity, he is at the final moment impeded by the principle of the material universe, symbolized in the various aspects of river, of wife, of matriarch. Blackness and frigidity are the leading attributes of this character—a principle opposed to man's search for his pristine simplicity. He is the angel in the poem, the bearer of the true spiritual whiteness, as opposed to the fleshy whiteness of the women.

Every poem of Rimbaud is in reality the microcosm of his complete story, and *Mémoire* seems to me his most dazzling performance. Nothing intervenes between the existence of the poem and the reader's sensitivity, the reader's own experience. No moral, no key can be exhumed from the verses. The story of *Mémoire* is the only story of man, the one continuing all the stories: a boy's flight from perdition, a solitary white angel of the spirit fleeing before all the black angels of the earth and the river.

Une Saison en Enfer:
The Poet's Destiny

Rimbaud began the composition of *Une Saison* in April 1873, when he was at Roche, a small village in the Ardennes, near Vouziers. There his family occupied a dilapidated house inherited from his maternal grandmother. He had just returned from London, exhausted by the excesses of his life there. His indulgence in tobacco,

alcohol, and hashish had fostered irritability, fever, and even hallucinations. A letter written from Roche in May to Ernest Delahaye
in Charleville states that he was working regularly on the new
piece, composed of brief stories in prose, to which he was giving
the general title: *Livre païen, ou Livre nègre* (Pagan book, or Negro
book).

This letter proves the importance attached to the new writing
and the belief that it marked a turning point in his life: "*Mon sort
dépend de ce livre pour lequel une demi-douzaine d'histoires atroces sont
encore à inventer*" ("My fate depends on this book, for which a half-
dozen atrocious stories are still to be invented"). He continued
intermittently to work on it after he went to London at the end of
May, and after Verlaine abandoned him in London to go to Brussels.
At the end of the July lawsuit (20 July 1873), Rimbaud, his arm in
a sling, returned to the farm at Roche and, using the attic as a
retreat, completed the work in the same place where he had begun
it five months earlier. It appeared in pamphlet form (in what the
French call *une plaquette*) in Brussels, in October (chez Poot et Cie,
37, rue aux Choux). Five hundred copies were printed, of which
Rimbaud received ten. These he distributed among friends. It has
often been written that the poet burned the remaining copies of the
edition in a desire to make more complete his flight from poetry,
but this is a false legend. The 490 copies remained closeted at the
printer's until 1901, when a Belgian bibliophile, Léon Losseau,
discovered them and bought them. Rimbaud had doubtless been
unable to pay the printing bill of this one book he himself wished
to publish.

Une Saison en Enfer is the metaphysical autobiography of Rimbaud, as well as a major text in the history of the modern spirit.
It appears to be a work of "confession," and like those of Saint
Augustine, Cellini, Montaigne, Rousseau, Chateaubriand, it involves other genres: autobiography, philosophy, psychology, history, theology. Rimbaud's confession differs from the others in its
brevity and in the explosive quality of its language, which makes
Une Saison almost a poem or a series of poems.

The violence of the work is not so much in the ideas and concepts
and facts as in the rhythms and movements of the phrases, in
the symbols that flash from the text not as commentary on the
experience but as the experience itself. A confession must necessar-
ily deal with the theme of evil, with the struggle of a single man
against the world of evil, and *Une Saison* is no exception. But it is
a strange narrative, where metaphysics takes first place of impor-

tance, and where the meaning of evil is converted into the meaning of action and the meaning of words. Poetry is the art where the articulation of a phrase, that is, the physical rhythm and breath of a phrase, is as vital as the actual meaning of the words in the phrase. This applies to so much of *Une Saison en Enfer*, where the meaning of suffering is communicated by means of the tempo—its violence and unevenness, its precipitation and delicacy, its blatancy and secretiveness—so that the work may be defined as the poem of a confession.

In this first section of *Une Saison*, "Mauvais Sang ("Bad Blood"), Rimbaud describes himself as being held to his past by singularly strong and inevitable bonds. He has inherited from his Gallic ancestors both physiological weaknesses and spiritual habits of thought that have determined and are continuing to fashion his drama. He is held by two kinds of past: the distant past of the sacrilegious, pagan Gauls and the immediate past of nineteenth-century bourgeois tradition, where each first son inherits his father's fortune and then transmits it to his son: *J'ai connu chaque fils de famille* (I have known the eldest son of every family). The inferior race of Gauls was quickly converted into medieval crusaders, and this created the three centuries of modern France, elliptically designated by Rimbaud with three words: *la raison, la nation et la science* (reason, the nation, and science). These were the landmarks of modern progress: reason in the seventeenth century, the nation in the eighteenth, and science in the nineteenth.

The poet sees himself first in all his roles of the past: leper, Gaul, crusader, son-heir. And then he sees himself in the future. The passage of pure prophecy is almost unprecedented in literature. Rimbaud foresees his flight from Europe (*je quitte l'Europe*) (I am leaving Europe), the deepening color of his skin under the tropical sun (*les climats perdus me tanneront*) (Lost climates will tan me), his return to Europe, with gold on his person (*Je reviendrai . . . J'aurai de l'or*) (I will come back . . . I will have gold), and his condition of being an invalid, nursed by women (*Les femmes soignent ces féroces infirmes retour des pays chauds*) (Women take care of these ferocious invalids from the torrid countries).

"*Adieu*," the last section in *Une Saison en Enfer*, is a farewell to autumn. Ahead lies the Mass of Christmas and the rebirth of purity. The cycle is completed, because the first sentence of *Une Saison* spoke of the wine of feast days and of the earliest child purity. The entire work is the narration of states of being between purity (*j'ai créé toutes les fêtes*) (I have created all celebrations) and sin (*la cité un ciel taché de feu*) (The city under a sky stained with fire), and finally repentance (*je dois enterrer mon imagination et mes souvenirs*) (I have to bury my imagination and my memories). The feast days of purification, the burning cities of Sodom and Gomorrah, and the dying of all nature at the end of autumn symbolize the major states of being in Rimbaud's life cycle. In the center of hell, Rimbaud remembered the birth of his purity in an ancient celebration and prophesied its rebirth in a future penitence.

Throughout his "season" he played his roles of magus and angel (*Moi qui me suis dit mage ou ange*) (I who called myself magus or angel), and now he knows his destiny is to be that of peasant (*paysan*).

Myth of Childhood

Rimbaud consecrated the child as a true hero in literature. The hero's new sensitivity is disengaged from the poem *Les poètes de sept ans* ("Seven-year-old poets"), at the same time as it relates the personal experience of all children in their initiation rite. At the end of childhood, in order to mark his entrance into the real world of men, the poet must undergo an initiation that will test his imagination and physical force. *Le grand Meaulnes* of Alain-Fournier, the narrator in Proust's novel, Stephen Dedalus in *A Portrait of the Artist*, the youthful acrobats of Picasso, the young girls of Marie Laurencin, the seventeen-year-old hero of *Brighton Rock* by Graham Greene, the rock singer-poet Jim Morrison*—all are reincarnations of Arthur Rimbaud, who maintains a child's vision of the world.

The poet Rimbaud resembles the little man-child of all ages: Papageno in Mozart's *Magic Flute*, or the youthful Miranda in *The Tempest*, who cries out in the middle of her dream:

> How beauteous mankind is! O brave new world
> That has such people in't. (V.1)

---

*The use of Rimbaud by rock musicians, especially by Jim Morrison of the Doors, is of interest to young people. Allow me to refer to my treatment of this subject in two of my memoir books: *Aubade: A Teacher's Notebook*, 174–76, and *Sites: A Third Memoir*, 163–73.

The new heroic role is lunar, a role consecrated by Rimbaud in his boy of the boat, who can seize neither the yellow nor the blue flower emerging from the water around him (*Mémoire*).

Within Rimbaud is the eternally young and impotent ancestor of many juvenile heroes who have appropriated for themselves the first place in modern art. He is one of Picasso's clowns, who in his acrobatics forms with his body a rose or a tree. He is the straw-stuffed body of Petrouchka. He is the terrible adolescents of Cocteau, equally those who throw snowballs and those who are wounded by the snowballs.

Rimbaud lives in the two boys of *Finnegans Wake*, in the two sons, Shem and Shaun, in whom James Joyce incarnates the two species of men. Shem is explorer, *voyant*, and poet. Shem is orator and prudent schemer who succeeds. In a children's game, Shem takes the role of the "bold bad bleak boy of story books," and Shaun, the role of the "fine frank fair-haired fellow of the fairy tales." These two alliterations, *bad boy* and *fine fellow*, describe the two roles of *voyou* and angel played by Rimbaud.

The progeny is numerous. At least in three novels of Iris Murdoch, the mark of Rimbaud is visible in three youths: in Leo Peshkov in *The Time of the Angels*, in Beautiful Joe of *Henry and Cato*, and in Titus of *The Sea, the Sea*.

The "irreconciliable," which the artist meets on various sociological and psychological levels, is always at the core of his major experience, explicitly so in Hart Crane, and also in Rimbaud, with whose poetry Crane felt strong affiliations, although he was unable to read it easily in the original. Their experience and temperament were so similar that there was little need for Crane to have a literal translation of Rimbaud's texts.

Between life and art there will always extend an abyss of physical and psychic anguish. "I meet you therefore in that eventual flame," Faustus says to Helen in Crane's poem, and thereby states the meeting between the poet and beauty, a meeting quite improbable without the flame of experience. Experience is the punishment for Crane and Rimbaud, and in that room of fire there is no peace and no canticle celebration of love.

There is a parallel in the desire of both poets to live with primitive peoples, in Rimbaud's return to the blacks of Africa, in Crane's visits to sailors' dives and Mexico. In the prophetic trances of his late adolescence, Rimbaud saw himself as a god among the Africans, and was in reality the slave to his own nature and an outcast from the bourgeois society of Charleville and Paris. Hart Crane, in the poems he wrote between the ages of twenty and thirty, saw himself as the artist in the midst of the normal bourgeois of Chicago and New York, and was in reality the clown among the sailors and the tough boys of the waterfront bars.

In the poetry of Rimbaud and Crane the image of a body of water, whether it be the sea or the river, is the persistent symbol of the universe. It is the cruelest of symbols, the mightiest and the most inhuman, the element of nature man is least able to embrace or comprehend: the imaginative experience of Rimbaud in his flight down the river to the fullness of the ocean, the bitterness he feels there in the expanse of depth and color, and his subsequent return, not to the river but to the caricature of water fertility, in the muddy pool of the city street.

The life story of Rimbaud in his escape from the ancient parapets of Europe to the countries of Africa and Asia, and his ultimate return to the hospital in Marseille, parallels the voyages in his literary testament. And likewise, the imaginative experience of Hart Crane, as related in *Atlantis*, the culminating section of *The Bridge*, where the sea subsumes all voices and all times, where we read the sea's drama formed by the extinguishing of other elements, parallels the literal experience of his suicide. The myth of Europe tortures Rimbaud and he tries to go behind it into pre-Christian, primal times. The myth of America that Crane tries to comprehend is not yet fully created.

The role of woman in a poet's work is closely associated with his feeling about the problem of good and evil. The poet's is the transformation of the universe into his own poetic universe. He counterfeits the essential gesture of the priest, and poetry, which is the changed substance, remains inviolate. The muse is perhaps simultaneously Eve and Our Lady. Neither saint nor profane, the muse resembles all women and is none of them. With Hopkins and Péguy she is the Virgin; with Rimbaud and Crane she is mystery, more explicitly than ever the muse, for the name was invented to disguise mystery and hide the imperishable impulse of man toward woman.

The mighty symbol of water surrounds and submerges especially those heroes who know that love is condemned and who seek an unknown holiness: Icarus, Prometheus, Rimbaud, Crane. The necessary bridge immobilized across the water is the religious statue for Crane. Rimbaud's boat is never moored, and at the end of its drunkenness its keel collapses and it sinks into the depths. Crane's suicide joined him to the major symbol of his poetry—the sea—in which he had sought as an artist a release and a sanctification, in which he ultimately found as a man an end to suffering and an escape from himself.

In *Une Saison en Enfer*, Rimbaud speaks of the Orient and of his return to the original wisdom of the East.

Je retournais à l'Orient et à la sagesse première et éternelle
("L'Impossible")

(I returned to the East and to the first eternal wisdom)

There are traces in his writings of Plato's idealism, traces also of the occult tradition, of the initiate in the cabalistic and alchemist tradition. But far more than in the fragmentary allusions to Plato and the occult, Rimbaud's knowledge of himself and of the world is to be found in the ancient discovery and practice of poetry.

Arthur Rimbaud was, at a very early age, a sufferer and a rebel. Charleville, where he grew up, was a stifling prison, the site of perpetual penance for him, where all the elements of authority— school, mother, and church—seemed ludicrous and bent upon crushing his spirit. His one escape was "vision"—that is what he calls it in *Les poètes de sept ans*—the willed discovery of an obscure world beyond the immediate world. He cultivated the moment of vision avidly, and those feelings grew until they forced him to leave Charleville abruptly, melodramatically, in an invincible need for freedom and purity. But he always had to return to Charleville, penniless and sheepish, and try to forget the escapes, as he walked in the streets of the city, read in the public library, or drank beer in the bistrots of the Place Ducale with his friends Delahaye and Bretagne.

As all the usual hostilities toward the world grew in Rimbaud, his personality as an adolescent grew into a closed universe. His poems were the spiritual struggle of his ego and at the same time the ancient effort of the human race to follow not the narrow confines of dogmatism but the freedom of thought.

"The reasoned derangement of all the senses" is the formula for this method and Rimbaud insists on its lengthiness and its vastness (*un long, immense et raisonné dérèglement de tous les sens*) (a long, gigantic, rational derangement of all the senses). It would be difficult to know what Rimbaud meant by *dérèglement* if he had not explained the word in the same passage of the *Lettre* by the three experiences of love, suffering, and madness. These are the aspects of violence, the derangements that train the soul and lead it to the "unknown," to that state of detachment from daily realities that deaden the soul. Violence was for Rimbaud a regimen of asceticism. In a moving letter to Delahaye, written from Paris from his room in the rue Monsieur-le-Prince, he describes in detail his regimen: an all-night vigil of study, the coming of dawn, his fasting, his descent into the street at the earliest moment when he could purchase bread, the return to his room, and finally, his sense of detachment from the city.

Rimbaud knew deeply and tragically the perils of exposure and the failures to which his mind was exposed. His first and only contact with the established Parisian writers was a disaster. He was rigorously excluded or admitted derisively. After the Brussels drama and the return to his mother's farm at Roche, in July 1873, Rimbaud was despondent, discouraged, humiliated. Most of *Une Saison en Enfer* was composed at that time. The text is a kind of morality play where reminiscences immediate and distant are juxtaposed with impulses to rebellion and outbursts of exuberance.

These are questions posed as themes throughout the text, and which became, later in the twentieth century, in the writings of the surrealists, poetic beliefs. Language, in its power of communication, is a return to a lost unity. Poetry is a means by which one man participates in the world.

Readings, memories, images picked up at random turn into visions. The poet indulges in a telescoping of words, taken out of context, and converts them into something monstrous. The combining of the real and the unreal in his writing makes it inexhaustible. A poem of Baudelaire is intact, self-contained, a closed metaphysical system. It is an art that has gone past the experimental stage and reaches the calculated effect within the limits of prosody and metaphor. A page of Rimbaud is more open. The music of the lines creates affinities between the parts. A poem of Baudelaire contains all that can be communicated from a given moment of the poet's consciousness. An *illumination* of Rimbaud is a force able to promote vision outside itself.

La vraie vie est absente, wrote Rimbaud in *Une Saison* (Real life is absent). Such a phrase is a new seizure of reality. It is not expressed logically. It is an opening out to systems and philosophies, to moments in Claudel's *Le Soulier de Satin* (The Satin Slipper), to Beckett's *Fin de Partie* (Endgame), to Breton's *Nadja*. The hard, reduced phrases of Rimbaud helped to cast into disrepute the traditional syllabic verse of French poetry. Since Valéry, few poets have used the alexandrine or decasyllabic line except Cocteau, from time to time, and Aragon. But Char, Ponge, Jacob, and Saint-John Perse are among those whose poetic form is reminiscent of *Les Illuminations*.

Rimbaud first, and especially in passages of *Une Saison*, taught that art is the antidote of the familiar, the habitual, even though he used familiar objects in his poems, as Picasso and Braque used them in their still-lifes. A boat speaks in his most famous poem, but the reader senses that this is no usual boat. By the end of the voyage, the boat has turned into a paper boat in a mud puddle, and the reader has moved far away from the familiar confines of his world.

Le Bateau Ivre was designed to trouble, to upset, to discontent. It is in opposition to the familiar relationships we establish or that have been established for us. And it creates new relationships for our mind that reveal unsuspected meanings that henceforth we will attach to such a commonplace object as a boat. *Le Bateau Ivre* illustrates the limitlessness of poetry. Poetry is what we habitually neglect, a world of vast proportions by comparison with the limited, contained world in which we live.

The word that seems out of its usual place in a poem of Rimbaud—in *Mémoire*, such words as *la soie en foule, la sphère rose, dragueur*—is there as an aid, as something we can hold on to, as to a buoy in the sea, as an island that is stable. The principle of the esoteric presides over all poetry, and the poet is knowing or unknowing of this principle. To give meaning is a magic process: the meaning of a drunken boat, of a flight from home, of a first communion, of a buffet, of the delousing of a boy's head of hair. The absolute is unintelligible from our limited viewpoint, but the poet plunges into it, utilizes it, and finds there his freedom and the game of poetry.

Rimbaud unquestionably felt the perils of this enterprise, of this plunge into the unknown, into the absolute, and the only sound explanation of his flight from literature is this sense of peril. He realized that poetry, which ultimately is the control of words, is initially the loss of control of a man's faculties. It is an experience of madness, an entrance into what Baudelaire called *la surnature*. It is impossible to estimate the scruples Rimbaud felt over the poetic experience that forced him to abandon it. Mallarmé's contemplation of the white page, of that wordless absolute, is comparable to Rimbaud's sterility that followed so closely upon his career as a poet.

6

Jules Laforgue:
Pierrot and Hamlet

Jules Laforgue called himself "un bon Breton né sous les tro-
piques." He was born in Montevideo. At the age of six, he was
brought to Tarbes in southern France, where, with his brother,
Émile, he attended the Lycée de Tarbes during several years of
intense solitude. The family moved to Paris in 1875, and Jules
finished his lycée years at Fontanes (called today Condorcet). He
took courses at the Ecole des Beaux-Arts, listened to Taine lecture,
and frequented museums and libraries, especially the Bibliothèque
Nationale. Some of his early poems date from 1875.

He was quite alone in Paris in 1880–81, when Charles Ephrussi,
an art historian of exceptionally fine taste, engaged in writing a
book on Dürer, hired him as secretary. Laforgue's life in Paris was
typical of the talented young provincial, in love with literature,
ambitious to become a writer, and leading a miserable solitary
existence.

A change came at the end of 1881. Ephrussi secured for Laforgue
the post of French reader to Empress Augusta of Germany. For five
years he lived in Berlin in a magnificent apartment in the royal
palace, *unter den Linden*. He had a personal servant and usually ate
with the ladies-in-waiting of the court. He resembled a clergyman in
his impeccable black suit. Whenever the empress traveled, Laforgue

followed the court—to Baden, Hamburg, Coblenz. He made a few friends in Berlin, where he studied German art and attended concerts, operas, and the circus.

After the five years in Germany, he married a young English girl in London, and then settled in Paris. Poverty and ill health again beset his last few years. He died at the age of twenty-seven, unable to secure enough funds to leave Paris for a warmer climate.

Laforgue felt all the principal literary influences of his day— Vigny, Hugo, Gautier, Balzac—but was most deeply affected by Baudelaire, Corbière, Rimbaud, and Mallarmé. He felt a close affinity with the type of sad Pierrot, a familiar symbol of the young Parisian intellectual of 1880. The prophetic tendency in him was curiously fused with the clown. He was exactly the type of hero, or artist-intellectual, whose psychology and drama he wanted to describe in his writing: the genius-failure.

Gradually Laforgue's work has been assuming a place of importance in the history of symbolism. The first really constituted group of symbolist poets was active from 1880 to 1885, years when Laforgue was absent for the most part from Paris and was writing his major poems. The word *"décadent"* has been associated with this particular group of poets (Moréas, Morice, Tailhade, Fénéon, Kahn). The decadent reacted against the platitudes of his day and opposed to them the unusual, the precious, the refined. Des Esseintes, hero of Huysmans's novel *A rebours*, was the leading type of decadent. Verlaine subscribed to the new emphasis. Gustave Kahn, who had maintained a correspondence with Laforgue in Germany, asked for contributions to *La Vogue*, a magazine he began publishing in April 1886.

To students of Laforgue today, the characters in his book, *Moralités légendaires* (1887)—Pan, Lohengrin, Hamlet, Salomé—appear as thinly disguised self-portraits rather than symbols of universal import. "Decadence," if it has any meaning at all, applies better to Laforgue than the term "symbolism." Baudelaire had taught Laforgue's generation significant lessons on self-analysis and on the morbid pleasure to be derived from such analysis. Paul Bourget, in his *Essais de psychologie contemporaine*, pointed out that *"décadent"* became the battle cry of the new school. He called it a *pessimisme parisien* that spread outside of France.

Laforgue's first poems, published after his death as *Le Sanglot de la Terre* (The Sob of the Earth) (1901), are the easiest to read and the most recognizable to readers of Baudelaire in their litanies of "spleen," and in the various exorcisms he practices to recover from spleen. There are many pictures of Paris, more localized and less universal than Baudelaire's, and cosmological visions in which the earth is seen as some abysmal mediocrity, a dying star in the vertigoes of universes.

The central image of *Le Sanglot de la Terre* is one of the heart—the heart of a solitary man, amassing so much remorse and adoration that it burns and bleeds like a rose window in a cathedral (*Rosace en vitrail*). The poet comes to read into this symbol of the hypertrophied heart the illusion of life. Laforgue is really considering the heart of the earth, and his poem is the passion of the earth, but his intelligence keeps a careful watch over his heart. No matter how cosmic his vision becomes, he always ends by parodying his own anguish. He is the type of passionate intellectual—"Hamlet without a sword," as Camille Mauclair called him—who refuses to take himself seriously and whose most heartfelt cries are always silenced by the clown's grimace. Not even the pessimistic philosophy of Schopenhauer, whose work Laforgue read in Paris, and that of Hartmann, whom he read later in Germany, prevented his writing verse that is essentially a parody of sensibility.

The second group of poems Laforgue wrote, and the first to be published, *Les Complaintes* (1885), represented a new aesthetics and a new philosophy. His new language he called more "clownish." His boldness in vocabulary and style gave the collection a complex, bizarre effect, a poetic laboratory of hundreds of unexpected combinations. Some of the "complaints" are semiphilosophical, such as the opening one, a propitiation addressed to the unconscious, in which the poet prays to be released from thought. It is a parody of the Lord's prayer:

> *Non, rien: délivrez-nous de la Pensée*
> *Lèpre originelle, ivresse insensée.*

> (No, nothing: deliver us from thinking
> Original leprosy, intoxication)

The complaint of daily living is the most poignant of all:

> *Ah! que la vie est quotidienne!*

> (Ah! how daily life is!)

Hurdy-gurdies, pianos, billboards, photographs, October days, and Sundays are themes of the incurable complaint. As far back as the poet can go in his memory, he has been something of a clown, something of a genius *manqué*:

> *Comme on fut piètre et sans génie . . .*

> (What a fool we were and without talent . . .)

"Almost at times the fool!" Eliot will say through his Prufrock.

The character Pierrot gradually came to life in the poetry of Laforgue, and with the group of poems called *Imitation de Notre Dame la Lune* Pierrot assumed first place, combining the irony and the metaphysics of the earlier poetry. He and the moon carry on a dialogue, under the protection of Gustave Kahn and the priestess Salammbô, to whom the work is dedicated. Through the sensibility of these lunar inhabitants, called Pierrots, Laforgue was describing his own sensibility. Like them, he wanted to become legendary before the beginning of the false ages.

Derniers Vers (Last Poems), a series of twelve poems, are meditations on love. Their setting is always the same: the slums and the suburbs of cities. The 816 lines appear almost as a continuous poem. There was nothing in the later Laforgue of the grand style of romantic poetry. He was concerned with depicting the shifts and variations of feelings in scenes of the modern city. Both the system of multiple allusions and the general atmosphere of spiritual sterility relate the work to *The Waste Land*. The dominant mood Laforgue expressed was one of emotional starvation and emotional inhibition. It was already the negative wit, the brevity of Prufrock.

The parody of his own sensibility became in Laforgue's *Moralités légendaires* the parody of some of the great myths of humanity. He recapitulated the stories of the masters—Shakespeare's Hamlet, Wagner's Lohengrin, Mallarmé's faun, Flaubert's Salomé—and he altered them in order to infuse new meanings into them. No such thing as a pure hero existed for Laforgue. He saw the so-called heroes as ordinary creatures, and gave them the psychological characteristics of his Pierrots—nervousness, anxiety, an ephemeral existence. By parody and anachronism, he created new characters out of the old. Each "morality" defined a concentrated action, a single crisis, which gave it a highly dramatic tone.

The most deeply hidden theme in his work, and probably the most important for an understanding of Laforgue as man and poet, is that of woman and love. He never concealed the anguish he felt over his celibacy. He was a recluse who was always depressed by his solitude. He feared not love but the deceit of love. He worried for fear that love was always a deceit of nature, and denounced what he believed to be the false myth of woman—very much the same myth Simone de Beauvoir denounced later in *Le Deuxième Sexe*, in which she quotes Laforgue. He spoke against the deification of woman, against the mystery with which she has been surrounded. Either he vituperated against what he believed was woman's falseness or he regretted plaintively the disappearance of man's comradeship with women, or a simple natural relationship between the sexes.

With Rimbaud, a different metaphysics of poetry came into prominence. On the whole the surrealists disapproved of Laforgue. "Lisez Rimbaud, ne lisez pas Laforgue" was their admonition. Jean Cocteau tells the story of Picasso, Max Jacob, and Apollinaire once shouting in the streets of Montmartre: "Vive Rimbaud! A bas Laforgue!"

Laforgue and T. S. Eliot

Whereas Ezra Pound praised Laforgue in lavish terms, Eliot remained always more cautious, anxious not to place Laforgue with the major poets—with Baudelaire, for example—or with Valéry. He did, however, acknowledge his debt to the French poet. "Laforgue was the first to teach me how to speak. I owe more to him than to any one poet in any language."

The dandies and the Pierrots in Laforgue's verse make him into the master of a self-accusing irony. This is the first Laforguian trait one discovers in Eliot's early verse. Prufrock was not meant to be Prince Hamlet. Hamlet in both Laforgue and Eliot is not up to his role.

Today, more in England and America than in France, Laforgue has a substantial place in literary history. There is thinness in his poems, and monotony in the inevitable recurrence of the themes of Sundays, of autumn, of rain, of piano playing. The women are girls in his verse, and the men conceal their inner passion under jokes and flashes of cruelty. He chose a minor kingdom, not as significant as a wasteland. But his influence was deeply felt in Eliot, first and foremost, and then in Wallace Stevens, who acknowledged a debt to Laforgue. Hart Crane translated some of Laforgue's poems. Eliot's early poems mark an improvement over Laforgue. There was at that time, according to Eliot, no English equivalent to Laforgue's language.

Les Complaintes of 1885 represented an innovation in language, syntax, and metrics. The ironic sentiments, the bouffoneries (*cocasseries*) he made fashionable, were reflected in the poetry of those poets who followed him: Apollinaire and Jacob in France and Eliot and Crane in America. His influence was fairly strong between 1890 and 1920, and after that moment Arthur Rimbaud took over as a far stronger influence on modern poetry.

Laforgue and Corbière are often named together as the two fore-runners of Eliot and Crane, as poets concealing under a mask of irony a need for affection. In 1940, in an article on Yeats, Eliot wrote, "The kind of poetry I needed, to teach me the use of my own voice, did not exist in English at all; it was only to be found in French." Eliot was a member of the Harvard class of 1910. His first poems that appeared in the *Harvard Advocate* were written in a Laforguian manner. In 1914 Eliot met Ezra Pound in London, who introduced him to the art of several French poets, but it seems to have been Eliot who taught Pound to admire Laforgue. e. e. cummings was at Harvard between 1914 and 1918. He passed on his discovery of Laforgue to Malcolm Cowley, who was at Harvard in 1920. In his book *Exile's Return* (1934), Cowley has described literary life in the 1920s and recorded a testimonial to the undercurrent of interest in French symbolist poetry existing at Harvard during those years.

After too many country poets, Laforgue's urban subject matter was a welcome change. The French poet's style of writing, with its irony and paradox and exhibition of learning, was also the style of Eliot. Malcolm Cowley called "The Love Song of J. Alfred Prufrock" the greatest example of a Laforgue poem. The French poet's attitude toward woman was one of hope, to find in her his happiness. But she can also appear to man as a witch who incarcerates man in a dungeon. (Rimbaud in one of his prose poems calls woman both *déesse* [goddess] and *sorcière* [sorceress]).

The "tangent ending" is a term used by Kenneth Burke as applicable to poems of Laforgue and Eliot where the poet unfolds a situation and then moves away from it at a tangent. During his tea-time visit to the ladies, Prufrock decides he will never find the courage to express his love. And then, abruptly, Prufrock imagines he is walking on the beach and listening to the mermaids. Prufrock is

Laforgue's brother when he speaks of the monotony of life, of the relentless passing of hours:

I . . . have known the evenings, mornings, afternoons,
I have measured out my life with coffee spoons.

Eliot learned from Laforgue and Corbière that humor can be a source of acceptable poetry. In a sense, Laforgue succumbed to the fate of an innovator, while Eliot became the far greater poet. Because of his verbal pyrotechnics, French critics tend to look upon Jules Laforgue as immature. They hesitated to accept his tone of irony. And yet Eliot adopted that tone and seemed to prove that irony can exist with poetry and may even enhance it.

The character of Hamlet in Shakespeare and in Laforgue's *Moralités légendaires* is presented, at least fleetingly, as a corruptor of women. For both poets Hamlet is an author, a "decadent" artist, as the nineteenth century would call him. And the *cabotin* too, the *histrion*, the mediocre actor, the man for whom acting has replaced action.

"Le décadent," as Laforgue uses the word, characterizes the young man in retreat from reality, from a world he is psychologically incapable of confronting. The French word *cabotinage* (ham acting) would seem to describe the essence of Hamlet in Laforgue's understanding of the character. It means a form of self-ridicule, a style of behavior close to our term "camp" as used today. Hamlet had grown into a mythic figure, and Laforgue's Hamlet is one aspect of that myth, stressing incongruity, an unwillingness to follow reasonableness and seriousness. There is a darker universe in Laforgue, however, in his Hamlet as well as in his Pierrots. A sense of abjectness is there, and loneliness and even terror. This aspect of the hero's character will be taken up and developed in the characters of Sartre, and especially in those of Samuel Beckett. The lineage is fairly clear today. It starts with Jules Laforgue, then passes through both Eliot and Joyce, and culminates with Beckett. It is the view of man as a being first ridiculous, and then, ultimately, tragic. Laforgue's title *Hamlet, ou les suites de la piété filiale* ("Hamlet, or the Consequences of Filial Piety"), might easily fit Beckett's second major play, *Fin de partie* (Endgame), where paternal and filial piety exists in Hamm and Clov.

Laforgue's Hamlet has ties with Shakespeare, with Pierrot, and with the court fool. Beckett's Hamm is related to Shakespeare's

Hamlet and to the ham actor, to Noah's ark and Noah's son Ham, after the flood, when no one is left on the earth. Laforgue's Hamlet and Beckett's Hamm are both writers, both heroes and antiheroes, both humorous and despairing, both heroes of the absurd.

The traits common to Laforgue and Beckett are many. A conversational tone is everywhere, even in emotional matters. Their emphasis on paradox is as strong as their use of parody and erudite allusions. *Humour noir* is a combination of laughter and terror, and this is used as frequently as *le monologue intérieur* (or "stream of consciousness"). The character-creatures of Laforgue are more refined, more graceful than Beckett's, but in both authors their creatures appear to be stationed on the edge of nothingness (*le néant*). The lords of their land are impotent and sterile. If they can be called characters in search of the absolute, the search is unconscious. They are beings thanks to the voice of the writer.

Jules Laforgue possessed a determined fidelity to his vocation, but I believe it can be said that he was unconvinced about everything else.

7

Tristan Corbière:
Resurrected Tristan

The first edition of Tristan Corbière's one book, *Les Amours Jaunes* (Yellow Loves), appeared in 1873, which was also the year of Rimbaud's *Une Saison en Enfer* and Verlaine's *Romances sans paroles* (Songs Without Words). Corbière died two years later, at the age of thirty. Not until 1883, in Verlaine's series of essays, *Les Poètes Maudits* (Poets Under a Curse), was Corbière presented to the Paris public as a poet of importance. This first label of *poète maudit* has remained associated with his name. He refused to write poetry in accordance with traditional forms. He even refused to be a traditional bohemian. "An ocean bohemian" Jules Laforgue once called him, since most of his life was spent in Brittany, in the towns of Morlaix and Roscoff, and since the themes of his personal suffering are mingled with the dominant theme of the sea.

In many ways Corbière was the spiritual descendant of François Villon, especially in his self-disparagement. He looked upon himself as a failure both as a man and poet, and he looked upon his life as a marriage with disaster. His early suffering seemed to come from the nostalgia of a youth who longed to be a sailor and whose ill health prevented him from becoming one.

Corbière's first poems, grouped under the title *Gens de mer* (Sea People) and placed at the end of his volume, celebrate the harmony existing between sailors and the natural forces they learn to control. His life of solitude and poor health forced him into the role of eccentric, which he took pleasure in exaggerating. The rheumatism from which he suffered altered his appearance when he was still very young. His body grew excessively thin, his complexion turned yellow, and his nose and ears appeared large in proportion to his face. His self-portrait is the sketch of a monster.

He ate always in the same restaurant in Roscoff, a café-pension called "Le Gad," where in summer he fell in with a convivial group of painters from Paris. This contact, which continued during several summers, influenced the cynicism and moral laxity of *Les Amours Jaunes*, the license in verbal expression, the puns, the care for picturesqueness, the need to shock.

Bohemianism was his climate, both in Roscoff and Paris, when he went on a few occasions to follow the girl with whom he had fallen in love. Marcelle was the mistress of a rich man who visited Roscoff. Corbière met the couple in "Le Gad" and was introduced as the "character" of the place. It was the spring of 1871, a few months after the end of the Franco-Prussian War. The strange idyll between Corbière and the beautiful Italian girl was in keeping with the poet's life and character. The misogynist-turned-lover could never believe for long that any woman was capable of loving him.

The admirable poem, *Le poète contumace* ("the defaulter poet [Contumacious]"), was inspired by Marcelle's departure from Roscoff in October 1871. It is in the form of a love letter or a long complaint in which Tristan Corbière assimilates himself with the medieval Tristan of legend, whose name he had chosen and whose story he had just reenacted. The two Tristans were sailors, Bretons, and victims of fate and passion

Corbière followed Marcelle to Paris in 1872, where his behavior was even more eccentric than in Roscoff. He seemed to take a perverse delight in exaggerating his ugliness and his traits of cruelty and stubbornness. Tristan Tzara, in the preface to his edition of *Les Amours Jaunes*, develops the theory that Corbière was acting the extreme pose of dandy and remembering the lycanthropy of Pétrus Borel in his efforts to startle the bourgeois by playing wolf and vampire. Not until the surrealists, fifty years later, recognized Corbière as one of their most authentic ancestors was any serious attention paid to his work.

There are strong reminiscences of Baudelaire in *Les Amours Jaunes* and Baudelairian traits in Laforgue's impenetrability and in his will to hide the deepest secrets of his heart. There are concetti and antitheses almost in Góngora's style, and rhythmical innovations and patterns that Verlaine later developed. An art of living preceded this new art of poetry, articulated in such a line as:

L'art ne me connaît pas, je ne connais pas l'Art.

(Art does not know me, I do not know Art.)

This would seem to mean that only when the strict conception of a poem as a work of art is abandoned will the poet really become the poet. Rhetorical devices and verbal clichés that form a serious defect in *Les Fleurs du Mal* are absent from *Les Amours Jaunes*. Yet Corbière's control of his art is less strong than Baudelaire's and Rimbaud's, and his revolt against order and convention is less metaphysical than Rimbaud's. His defiance, his insolence, and even his obscenity are traits of the *poètes maudits*, one of the lost children in revolt who differed from the other major poets of the nineteenth century in France only in the degree of intensity and hopelessness that characterized their human drama. The despair that is the basis of Tristan Corbière's poetry comes from his feelings of having made some fatal alliance with a cause or malediction he is unable to define clearly.

Society was only slightly perturbed by the waywardness and idiosyncrasies of the *poètes maudits* because their lives were far less revolutionary than their writings. They rejected a certain orderliness in man's human destiny that had held sway for centuries, and they felt that in order to reach the new salvation, they had to risk damnation. Corbière has often been compared to Villon, and there are many linguistic and thematic traits in the two works to justify this comparison. But in a deeper, more metaphysical sense, they are almost antithetical. The wretchedness of man's fate and of his daily occupations is clearly in evidence in Villon and Corbière, but such disaster in Villon is never considered without its relationship to the poet's religious faith and hope.

The poet's defiance of God, the Luciferian attitude of Baudelaire and Rimbaud, have no place in Corbière's writing. The creature's torment is all the greater because of the absence of God. His self-debasement seems total as he passes from one phase to another—his failure in being a sailor or an adventurer or a lover. The first writers to comment on Corbière's art, men like Léon Bloy and Laforgue, Remy de Gourmont and Huysmans, all spoke of his failure as a poet. But today his verses seem as solid and permanent and deliberately articulated as those of the best technicians. A Corbière poem limps and breaks off and recovers when the poet wishes it to express the corresponding sentiment. His range in feeling and style permitted him to move from a disarming tenderness to a coarse joke. He felt closest to those Bretons pursued by bad luck, the invalids and the criminals he saw in the *Pardon de Sainte-Anne*, and who seemed to him an extension of himself. He was refused by the sea as he was refused by love, and most of his poems speak of those two experiences.

The sixty lines of *Epitaphe* are the portrait of one man's life. They are sixty examples of contradictions by means of which Tristan Corbière states, without analyzing them, the facets of his destiny—sixty incomprehensible states of being that set him apart from all other men. He calls his life an "adulterous mixture of everything" (*Mélange adultère de tout*). Each possibility is canceled out by its negative-opposite:

> *Coureur d'idéal—sans idée*
> (Seeker of the ideal—without an idea)
> *Artiste sans art*
> (Artist without art)
> *Acteur—il ne sut pas son rôle*
> (Actor—who did not know his role)
> *Très mâle—et quelquefois très fille*
> (manly—and at times girlish)
> *Incompris—surtout de lui-même.*
> (Misunderstood—especially by himself)
> *Ne croyant à rien, croyant tout*
> (Believing in nothing, believing everything)
> *trop réussi—comme raté*
> (too successful—as a failure)

To these we should add the most telling, the most desolate image of the poem:

> *Epave qui jamais n'arrive*
>
> (Flotsam that never reaches the shore)

T. S. Eliot borrowed the line *Mélange adultère de tout* for the title of one of his French poems, and makes up his own composition of contrasts and contradictions. They are more humorous than those of Corbière. The paradoxical qualities of the poet's temperament and the paradoxical mutations in the poet's career are quasi-tragic in Corbière and quasi-cynical in Eliot. Here are a few examples of Eliot's catalogue, so easily identifiable with Corbière's *Epitaphe*:

> *En Amérique, professeur;*
> *En Angleterre, journaliste;*
> . . . .
> *A Londres, un peu banquier,*
> . . . .
> *C'est à Paris que je me coiffe*
> *Casque noir de jemenfoutiste.*

> (In America, a professor
> In England, a journalist
> In London, something of a banker
> In Paris, a scoffer)

Corbière's life was far more restricted: Brittany to Paris, then briefly in Italy, and back to Brittany. Eliot's life, more varied, more exotic, extended in his imagination from Damascus to Omaha.

Corbière's fate has been that of being admired, first by Verlaine (in *Poètes Maudits* of 1883), and then subsequently in France by Apollinaire and the surrealists; and to be admired abroad by Eliot, Pound, and Hart Crane.

Discussion still continues today on the meaning of Corbière's title *Les Amours Jaunes*. Littré calls *jaune* (yellow) the color of Judas, the color representing betrayal. Was Marcelle's kiss to Tristan a Judas kiss? Yellow would apply to the love poems and to the poet's life in general, since he refers to his life as being unjust and unjustifiable. He was betrayed by life. By refusing to use the noble lyric tone of a Baudelaire, both Laforgue and Corbière revived (perhaps from Villon) the tone of humble acceptance in poetry. Even if their mask of irony concealed their need for affection, Laforgue in his poem says more simply what Corbière says throughout *Epitaphe*:

> *Je puis mourir demain et je n'ai pas aimé.*

> (I can die tomorrow and I have not loved.)

With some reason, Ezra Pound hailed Corbière as "the most poignant writer since Villon."

While admiring his father for the man's accomplishments as a novelist, Tristan Corbière felt crushed by his robust, virile old age and by his prestige as an adventurer and writer. He dedicated *Les Amours Jaunes* to his father, who never understood his son's poetry. Edouard Corbière, if the style of his writing had been less conventional, might have become a French Joseph Conrad.

Tristan was exiled from an active life as early as his lycée years in Nantes. His rheumatism and breathlessness (*essoufflement*) began at that time and continued thereafter to grow worse. These afflictions made his dream of becoming a sailor and a lover impossible. There were no violent scenes between him and his father. As a boy and as an adolescent he simply avoided his father by living in Roscoff, which had a gentler climate than Morlaix, where his family continued to live. He ceased being Edouard-Joachim Corbière and became Tristan, the Breton name he chose for himself and for his dog. The suffering and nostalgia in his poems are explicable on one simple level: they form the song of a boy who wants to be a sailor and who is not allowed to go on board ship.

In his one book Corbière grouped his poems in the reverse order of their composition. *Gens de mer*, his early poems, are placed at the end of the volume. They are filled with nostalgia for the virility of sailors and with hate for the shore to which he is bound.

The contemporary Breton poet Charles Le Goffic has told us that the name Corbière means in maritime language an extreme coastline, a path used by smugglers. Tristan was attracted to the poorest part of Brittany, the flattest part of the province, bristling with calvaries, without trees and harvests, a land of shipwrecks and burners of seaweed. That Brittany, not celebrated by Chateaubriand, was in close harmony with the personal distress of the poet.

Each summer, in 1872, 1873, and 1874, Marcelle and her lover, Rodolphe, returned to Roscoff, and each summer the painful idyll was played out. When Tristan went to Paris in the winter, where he rented a studio in close proximity to his love, Marcelle was ashamed of being seen with him. There in Paris, in 1873, he published at his own expense *Les Amours Jaunes*, his homage to Marcelle, who, after all is said, may have loved him. In December 1874 he was found unconscious in his room in Paris. Four months later, on 1 March 1875, he died in Morlaix.

His early commentators—Verlaine, Léon Bloy, Huysmans, Remy de Gourmont—referred to Corbière's strange syntax and to the awkwardness of his lines. Today his art seems both firm and supple to us, bolder than the art of his contemporaries. He could use a classical mold when he wished that. He could use a short line as skillfully as Charles d'Orléans. A line now and then seems pure Mallarmé. He was an able craftsman. The typographical appearance of his page prefigures Apollinaire and Marinetti. There is nothing abstract in *Les Amours Jaunes*, made up of noise, sobs, sperm, blood, objects, the sea, lighthouses. Yet his poems are not a Parnassian art, despite the fact that he was from time to time a painter, designer, and lithographer.

Corbière is most personal when he reproduces the surge and rhythm of the sea. At those moments he is close to Hugo and Baudelaire. In his Paris poems he often recalls Daumier and Courbet.

A prisoner of his very nature, he is the supreme example of a *poète maudit*. He celebrates a malediction, a mysterious curse placed on him. The word *épave* (used in *Epitaphe*), meaning flotsam or wreckage cast onto the shore, is his key word. His self-portraits are caricatures where he shows himself to be a confirmed sailor, the Breton who is happiest when he is cursing and drinking with sailors. He tells us that he died expecting to live (*Il mourut en s'attendant vivre*), and he lived expecting to die (*Et vécut s'attendant mourir*).

Emile Henriot, in his book *De Lamartine à Valéry* (1946), points to Corbière as a prefiguration of Rimbaud's *Bateau Ivre*. Born nine years after Corbière, Rimbaud never met him and probably never read *Les Amours Jaunes*. The critics have paid far less attention to Corbière than to Rimbaud. There is still need for a more careful assessment of the power of Corbière's apostrophes, oaths, proverbs, of the sense he gives us of the sea and of the Middle Ages.

In a short poem of twelve lines, *Ronde*, Corbière calls the child "thief of sparks":

Il fait noir, enfant, voleur d'étincelles

(It is night, child, thief of sparks)

Instinctively one recalls the Rimbaud phrase in his letter of 15 May:

je me suis fait voleur de feu.

(I turned into a fire thief.)

8

Paul Verlaine:
Symbolism and Decadence

*P*aul Verlaine used the term *poète maudit* for Corbière, Mallarmé, Rimbaud—and for himself.

Of the three major poets following Baudelaire and continuing his poetic practice—Verlaine, Rimbaud, and Mallarmé—Verlaine is the easiest and the most accessible today. His poems are the most frequently memorized by young readers, especially in France, but in other countries as well, wherever French is studied.

Verlaine wanted to be recognized as the poet who continued the tradition begun by Baudelaire, as the poet who best upheld the liberation announced by Baudelaire and the right of the modern poet to say everything and to suggest everything. The extraordinary musical effects of his verses place him in a category by himself:

> De la musique avant toute chose

> (Music before everything else)

he writes in the opening of his *Art Poétique*, a line that may have been inspired by the opening line of Shakespeare's *Twelfth Night*:

> If music be the food of love, play on.

Sixteen of his poems have been set to music by Debussy, and several poems were used by Gabriel Fauré and Renaldo Hahn.

In comparison with the poetic output of Mallarmé, who published little through an excess of scruples, and with the output of Rimbaud, who gave up writing poetry at twenty, Verlaine published too much too quickly. The musical beauty and the simplicity of his best poems are in marked contrast, and even in contradiction, to the complexity of his nature, of his personality, of his life story.

He would seem to be the rebel: in his early escape from school, in deserting his wife and child, in his travels and cohabitation with Rimbaud. But he was not at all the real rebel. He was unstable and wavering in everything: in the places where he lived, in the plans he made to earn his living, in his intentions, in his sentiments. He qualifies as an excellent example of the split personality, of the *homo duplex*, in his coarse sensuality and his tenderness. How to reconcile these opposing drives was, in a way, the drama of his life. Born under the planet Saturn, he illustrated the characteristics of the Saturnian: coldness in mood and gloomy in disposition. His first book acknowledges this heritage, *Les Poèmes Saturniens* (1866), influenced by Baudelaire's apostrophe concerning *Les Fleurs du Mal: jette ce livre saturnien* (throw away this Saturnian book).

Born in Metz in 1844, Verlaine was brought to Paris at the age of seven, in 1851. He won the baccalaureate at eighteen. Excessive drinking soon became a major problem, and absinthe led to hallucinations and delirium tremens. *Les Fêtes Galantes* (Amorous Celebrations) of 1869, more than his first volume of poems, made him famous. The paintings of Antoine Watteau and the characters from the *commedia dell'arte* were the inspiration for those twenty-two poems.

In 1870 Verlaine married Mathilde Mauté. She was sixteen and Verlaine was twenty-six. When Rimbaud arrived in 1871, invited by Verlaine, Mathilde was pregnant. The young rebel from Charleville (Rimbaud was seventeen) broke up the marriage. When the two poets left together for London and Belgium, the young wife initiated a suit of separation (*procès de séparation*).

At the end of the brief liaison, when they were living in Brussels, Verlaine shot Rimbaud. One of the two bullets wounded Rimbaud's left wrist. As a result of this escapade, Verlaine spent two years in Belgian prisons, first in Brussels and then in Mons (1873–75). They were not unhappy years. As he encouraged in himself a seemingly sincere sense of remorse, he read widely and composed new poems, some of which are among his best. He was in prison when he reached his thirtieth birthday.

The victim of the Verlaine-Rimbaud couple was Verlaine, the older man. The story would not have been related so often, and in so many varying ways, if they had not been authentic poets. When facing the judge in the Brussels court, both Rimbaud and Verlaine denied that they had engaged in homosexual acts. Since the middle of the century, our world, favoring scenes of violence and rock music, has preferred Rimbaud the executioner to Verlaine the victim.

The temperaments of the two poets were as opposed as Caliban and Ariel in *The Tempest*. Rimbaud was fundamentally unsociable, pitiless, and diabolically scornful of the weaker Verlaine. Their last meeting took place in 1875, in Stuttgart, at night, on the banks of the Neckar River. The effort at reconciliation ended in a fistfight, with Rimbaud knocking Verlaine to the ground and leaving him stretched out on the grass of the riverbank. It was the farewell scene. Rimbaud then took off for further voyages and thus converted the adventure into a parable that he describes in *Une Saison en Enfer*, when he calls himself "the infernal bridegroom" (*L'Epoux infernal*) and Verlaine "the foolish virgin (*La Vierge folle*).

Verlaine appears today as the leader of a school of poetry, of one aspect of symbolism. Picasso, in his sketch of Verlaine's face, makes him into a sad, obscene aging clown, the face of a faun possibly, or of Socrates. As a technician, Verlaine liberated the classical line, the somewhat rhetorical line of French poets, by condemning what he called "eloquence" and by advocating shadings of color rather than the full color (*la nuance, pas la couleur*).

Les Fêtes Galantes, Verlaine's collection of twenty-two poems, demonstrates an exceptional artistic unity, largely under the inspiration of Watteau, two of whose paintings had been on exhibition in the Louvre since 1870: *Gilles* and *L'Indifférent*. Baudelaire named Watteau in his poem *Les Phares* ("The Beacons") and in several places in his art criticism.

The final poem in the collection, *Colloque sentimental* ("Sentimental Dialogue"), is the narration of a bare tragedy. Two phantom figures of a man and woman pass through a frozen park in winter and try to recall their love when they had been alive. Their love is over, despite the efforts of one to evoke the romantic incidents of their experience. This poem of ghostly lovers was used by the filmmaker Duvivier in *Le Carnet de bal* (The Dance Card) of 1937.

All the poems of *Les Fêtes Galantes* form a comedy reminiscent of the characters, gestures, sentiments, and settings of the *commedia dell'arte*. A vague, ill-defined sadness is expressed (or mimed) throughout. It is the tone of the first poem, *Clair de lune* ("Moonlight"), that becomes the clearer tone of tragedy in the final poem, *Colloque sentimental*. Behind the banal gestures of lovemaking a pessimistic indifference to love is audible.

In his cell in the prison in Mons in 1873, Verlaine wrote a seemingly slight poem beginning with the words: *Le ciel est, pardessus le toit*. In its rapid succession of notations it gives a typically Verlainian impression of *rêverie*, which is far more poignant than lighthearted. The perfect poem, taken from the collection *Sagesse* of 1881, is memorized by French schoolchildren as easily as they memorize La Fontaine's fables and Ronsard's love sonnets.

The poet looks through the bars of his Belgian cell and sees the blue sky and a tree waving its branches:

> *Le ciel est, pardessus le toit,*
> *Si bleu, si calme!*
> *Un arbre, par-dessus le toit,*
> *Berce sa palme.*

> (The sky is, above the roof,
> So blue, so calm!
> A tree, above the roof,
> Waves its palm leaf.)

In the second stanza we hear two sounds, that of a bell ringing and a bird singing:

> *La cloche dans le ciel qu'on voit,*
> *Doucement tinte.*
> *Un oiseau sur l'arbre qu'on voit*
> *Chante sa plainte.*

> (The bell in the sky one sees,
> Softly rings.
> A bird in the tree one sees
> Sings his lament.)

Then he hears, coming from the town, sounds of family happiness:

Mon Dieu, mon Dieu, la vie est là,
  Simple et tranquille,
Cette paisible rumeur-là
  Vient de la ville.

(God, my God, life is there,
  Simple and quiet.
That peaceful murmur there
  Comes from the town.)

There is obviously a pause after the third stanza. Someone speaks to the poet (is it God or his conscience?) as he weeps in his cell and asks what he had done with his youth. (Verlaine was almost thirty when he wrote this poem.)

Qu'as-tu fait, ô toi que voilà,
  Pleurant sans cesse,
Dis, qu'as-tu fait, toi que voilà,
  De ta jeunesse?

(What have you done, you in there,
  Weeping ceaselessly,
Tell me, you in there,
  with your youth?)

This poem, as so many of the circumstances in the life of Verlaine that had led up to it, encourages critics to compare Verlaine with Villon in the fifteenth century and the beginning of *Le Grand Testament: En l'an trentième de mon âge* (in the thirtieth year of my age). Each poet was concerned with drawing up in his poem a balance sheet (*un bilan*) of his past.

   In 1884 Huysmans, in his novel *A rebours*, discusses Verlaine's position in French poetry, and there tends to call him a *décadent* rather than a *symboliste*. Today Verlaine's technical skill is studied more fervently than his life story. But the picture of Verlaine the sad clown persists. His alcoholism, his homosexuality, and the passivity of his nature are still rehearsed as critics state, and then try to understand, his position as the most popular of the French symbolists. He found his master in the adolescent Rimbaud, and together they scandalized a few Londoners. After the Brussels drama, the poetry of Verlaine, in *Sagesse*, for example, became more and more spiritual. At the end of his life he appeared as a great poet fallen from grace. Yet he was consecrated by the other poets of Paris *"le Prince des poètes."* He died, deserted by all, in a hovel in the rue Descartes. A funeral mass was celebrated at Saint-Etienne-du-Mont, and he was buried in the cimetière des Batignolles.

La Décadence

Decadence in literature has a long history. In the *Satiricon,* Petronius speaks of the vices of a civilization that is celebrating its gradual death. Pessimism was more than a fashionable attitude in Verlaine's time. It was a philosophical theme in those poems of Verlaine where melancholy is almost a disease. Around his name in particular the legend of decadent writers was created and grew to include such complex meanings as neurotic, morbid, and perverse. Théophile Gautier, in a preface he wrote for the 1869 edition of *Les Fleurs du Mal,* speaks of *époques de décadence.* The word has an aggressiveness about it that was quickly picked up by journalists. The title of Verlaine's two volumes of criticism, *Les Poètes Maudits,* of 1883 and 1884, became an easy synonym for *les poètes décadents.* The attitude of the *décadent* toward society was more disgust than rebellion. The sense of monotony of daily life (Laforgue's *vie quotidienne*) made the decadent poet appear more maladapted to his society than the romantic poets a generation earlier. He felt and expressed the weariness of living and the boredom of provincial life that today we read of in Flaubert. The nascent desires in a man that might have made him into a heroic figure are quickly repressed by the hundred constraints that society imposes on him.

The active decadents formed small groups in order to protest against the way of life of an older generation. Their odd way of dressing was in itself a protest. The names with which they baptized their clubs threatened the more traditional aspects of society:

Hydropathes	(hydrogen sufferers)
Hirsutes	(hairy coarse fellows)
Zutistes	(scorners)
Jemenfoutistes	(don't-give-a-damners)

Their manifesto appeared in their magazine *Le décadent* in 1886 (10 April). It claimed that the decadents were born from a civilization imbued with the philosophy of Schopenhauer. They were not a literary school. Their mission was not to found something. They were there to destroy, to eliminate all the old banalities of tradition. These banalities were religion, social customs, justice—everything that was collapsing. They parodied Nerval, Baudelaire, Mallarmé, Verlaine. Laforgue they classified as both a decadent and a symbolist.

One author, Robert de Montesquiou, seemed to incarnate all the traits of the new type of decadent. He was, according to all accounts, a dandy, a roué, an eccentric in his behavior, a mystifier, a dilettante. He is a character in Huysman's *A rebours*, and he is a leading model for Charlus in Proust's novel.

The word *maudits* in Verlaine's title *Poètes Maudits* (*Poets Under a Curse*) is an aggressive word. The three poets he treats first—Corbière, Rimbaud, and Mallarmé—are those repulsed by civilization because they go against the established order of things: against morality and aesthetics. Corbière he sees as the scoffer, the poet in love with the sea, who ends by being thrown to the sharks. He calls Corbière the first revolutionary (*premier révolté*). Rimbaud is described by Verlaine as the poet of "remarkable strength" (*force splendide*). In his essay on Mallarmé, Verlaine stigmatizes as fools those who treat the poet as a fool. These three poets are free men united together in a revolt against logic, naturalism, and stupidity.

In 1884, the same year *Les Poètes Maudits* was being read, Huysmans published *A rebours* and gave in his protagonist Des Esseintes a man illustrating all the characteristics of decadence as understood at that time. Des Esseintes is an olfactory. In the sense of smell he discovers an unknown universe of sensations out of which he is able to create symphonies of perfumes. In the novel itself he discusses the decadent literature of Petronius (*Satiricon*) and the traits of decadence in such moderns as Baudelaire and Poe, Corbière and Verlaine, and Mallarmé in his prose poems.

During the early period of "decadence," an attitude of pessimism was fashionable. The character Des Esseintes, the operas of Richard Wagner, the philosophy of Schopenhauer, all contributed to this state of moral crisis. Wagner died in 1883. *La Revue Wagnérienne* was founded in February 1885 in Paris by Edouard Dujardin. The term "wagnérisme" became a close synonym of pessimism and decadence. The poems of Verlaine, frequently recited in cafés and cabarets, underscored a melancholy bohemianism that fused easily with decadence. Both Barrès and Bourget claimed that the legend of decadence was created around the name of Verlaine. Journals in

Paris and the provinces tended to mock the new school. It was named *le mal de fin de siècle* in memory of the earlier *mal du siècle* of romanticism.

The two collections of essays of Paul Bourget, *Essais de psychologie contemporaine* (1885), are still today penetrating studies of the moral life in France as it is reflected in literature ten or fifteen years after the Franco-Prussian War. The young writer at that time repressed the same social constraints, turned inwardly, and expressed strong traits of introversion and narcissism. He believed that industry, the growing force of industrialism, would eventually eradicate the personality of a man.

Pride, as expressed in romantic literature, in Byron's Manfred and in Vigny's Moïse, changed into Baudelaire's "spleen" and the pessimism of 1885. Whereas the writers of the generation of 1830 frequented the *salons*, participated in politics, and used in their poems the great lyric themes of love, nature, and death, the writers of 1885 wrote of the weariness of living, of their obsession with fate, and of the boredom of provincial life. Baudelaire in *L'Invitation au voyage*, Mallarmé in *Brise Marine*, and Verlaine in *Les Fêtes Galantes* describe the nostalgia they feel for another, less real world than that of Paris.

If Verlaine's human experience and suffering seem beyond our comprehension because they are so personal, we are better able to follow his poetic transcription of those experiences. His poem on the adventure with Rimbaud, *Crimen amoris* ("Crime of Love"), makes it resemble a marriage of heaven and hell. It is a theological explanation by a poet who for the first time perhaps understands the meaning of remorse and integrates it within his nature.

During his last years Verlaine was looked upon by many as the greatest living poet. In France, he is still one of the few poets who have reached the general public. His influence on the development of French poetry has been slight, despite the fact that he exploited brilliantly the resources of the French language. Today he is associated with impressionism. When a critical judgment is now made on Verlaine, it usually asserts his incapacity to move beyond a transitory and subjective impression of his themes.

9

The Legacy of Symbolism

E ver since the rich period of symbolism, in fact, ever since the work of the two leading forerunners of symbolism, Nerval and Baudelaire, French poetry has been obsessed with the idéa of purity. To achieve poetry in a "pure state" has been the persistent ambition of a century of literary, and specifically, poetic, endeavor. The ambition is to create poetry that will live alone by itself and for itself. In a deep sense, it is poetry of exile, narrating both the very real exile of Rimbaud from Charleville and from Europe and Mallarmé's more metaphysical exile within his favorite climate of absence. In this effort of poetry to be self-sufficient and to discover its end in itself, it has appropriated more and more pervasively throughout the span of one hundred years the problem of metaphysics. As early as Nerval, who actually incorporated the speculations of the eighteenth-century *illuminés*, poetry has tried to be the means of communication between man and the powers beyond him. Nerval was the first to point out those regions of extreme temptation and extreme peril that have filled the vision of the major poets who came after him.

This search for "purity" in poetic expression is simply a modern term for the poet's will of all ages to break with the daily concrete life, to pass beyond the real and the pressing problems of the moment. Poets have always tended to relegate what may be called "human values" to novels and tragedies or to their counterparts in earlier literary periods. Poetry is the crossroads of man's intelligence and imagination, from which he seeks an absolute beyond himself. That is why the term "angelism" has been used to designate the achievement and failures of the modern poets, especially those of Rimbaud and Mallarmé. Baudelaire called the poet "Icarus," and Rimbaud called him "Prometheus, fire stealer." The progressive spiritualization of modern art in all its forms is its leading characteristic. It brings with it a mission comparable to that of the angels, and also a knowledge of pride and defeat, which, strikingly, is the most exact characterization of some of the great poetic works of our day. Defeat of one kind is in Mallarmé's faun and in his *Igitur*. Claudel, in discussing *Igitur*, called it a "catastrophe." Defeat of another kind is in the long literary silence of Rimbaud after his twentieth year. And still of another kind, there is defeat in most of the poetry of the surrealists, who found it impossible to apply their poetic theory rigorously to their actual poems.

The example of Mallarmé's art was never considered so fervently and piously as during the decade 1940–50. His lesson is the extraordinary penetration of his gaze at objects in the world and the attentive precision with which he created a world of forms and pure relationships between the forms. His will to abstraction isolated the object he looked at, and his will of a poet condensed the object into its essence and therefore into its greatest power of suggestiveness.

The object in a Mallarmé poem is endowed with a force of radiation, with a force that is latent and explosive. The irises, for example, in *Prose pour des Esseintes*, have reached a "purity," from which every facile meaning has been eliminated. Such flowers as these come from the deepest soil of the poet's consciousness and emotions. They retain in their "purity," exempt as they are from all usual responses, the virtue of their source in great depths of consciousness and dreams. Their purity is their power to provoke the multiple responses of the most exacting readers, those who insist that an image appear in its own beauty, isolated from the rest of the world and independent of all keys and obvious explanations. Whatever emotion, whatever passion, was at the source of the poem, it has been forgotten in the creation of the poem. Poetry makes no attempt to describe or explain passion—that is the function of the prose writer, of the novelist; rather the object or image is charged with the burden of the literal experience. The image becomes the experience, but so changed that it is no longer recognizable.

The metaphor is an image endowed with a strange power to

create more than itself. Mallarmé's sonnet on the swan caught in the ice of a lake, *"Le vierge, le vivace et le bel aujourd'hui,"* illustrates the power of metaphor to establish a subtle relationship between two seemingly opposed objects in the world: a swan and a poet. The relationship is not stated in logical, specific terms, but it is implied or suggested or evoked by the metaphor. The reader's attention is fixed on the swan, as it is almost never fixed on an ordinary object in the universe. This attention that the metaphor draws to itself becomes something comparable to a spiritual activity for the reader, as it had once been for the poet. The poet's consciousness is contained within the metaphor. When the metaphor is an image of a sufficiently general or collective meaning, it becomes a myth, not merely establishing a relationship with another object but translating some aspect of man's destiny or man's nature. It is often difficult to draw a clear distinction between a metaphor and a myth, as in the case of Mallarmé's swan, who testifies to a basic human struggle and defeat.

Today, almost a century after Rimbaud's death, his fame is higher than ever and the influence of his poetry is felt everywhere. Editions of his work multiply each year. More than five hundred books about him have been written in all languages. Perhaps never has a work of art provoked such contradictory interpretations and appreciations. One hears of his legend everywhere, and underneath the innumerable opposing beliefs, one continues to follow the legend and conceal whatever drama tormented him. He was the adolescent extraordinarily endowed with sight and equally endowed with speech. But with the advent of manhood he deliberately desisted from the prestige of letters and a poet's career. The period of wonderment about his life and his flight from literature is just about over now. In its place, the study of the writings themselves is growing into its own, and it is obvious that their mystery far exceeds the actual language of his writings. With Mallarmé's, it forms the most difficult work to penetrate in French literature and the most rewarding to explore, because for both poets the act of poetry was the act of obedience to their most secret drama.

The work of Rimbaud is far more knowable than his life, but in his case especially, the one cannot be dissociated from the other. The example of his human existence has counted almost as much as the influence of his writing. Breton named him a surrealist because of his life story. Rivière named him the supreme type of innocent. In all justice it must be noted that Breton modified his earlier view and called Rimbaud an apostate, one who renounced his discoveries and called them "sophisms." Nerval's suicide and Lautréamont's total disappearance would please the surrealists more than Rimbaud's final choice of another kind of life than that of poetry.

Rimbaud's example will remain that of the poet opposing his civilization, his historical moment, and yet at the same time revealing its very instability, its quaking torment. He is both against his age and of it. By writing so deeply of himself, he wrote of all men. By refusing to take time to live, he lived a century in a few years, throughout its minute phases, rushing toward the only thing that mattered to him: the absolute, the certainty of truth. He came closest to finding this absolute in his poet's vision. That was "the place and the formula" he spoke of and was impatient to find, the spiritual hunt that did not end when the prey was seized.

Rimbaud's is the drama of modern man, as critics have often pointed out, by reason of its particular frenzy and precipitation, but it is also the human drama of all time, the drama of the quest for what has been lost, the unsatisfied temporal existence burning for total satisfaction, for total certitude. Because of Rimbaud's universality, or rather because of poetry's universality, the Charleville adolescent can seemingly appropriate and justify any title: metaphysician, angel, *voyou*, seer, reformer, reprobate, materialist, mystic.

The poet, as Rimbaud conceived of him, is, rightfully, all men. He is the supreme savant. The private drama of one boy, which fills the poignant pages of *Une Saison en Enfer*, is always deepened into the drama of man, tormented by the existence of the ideal he is unable to reach. And likewise, the pure images of *Les Illuminations*, which startle and hold us through their own intrinsic beauty, were generated and formed by a single man in the solitude of his own hope to know reality.

For the role of magus and prophet for the poet, so histrionically played by Victor Hugo, was substituted the role of magician, incarnated not solely by Rimbaud (whose *Lettre du voyant* of 1871 seems to be its principal manifesto) but by Nerval and Baudelaire, who preceded him, by his contemporary, Mallarmé, and by his leading disciples, the surrealists, thirty years after his death: Robert Desnos and René Char. This concept of the poet as magician dominates most of the poetic transformations and achievements of the last century. The poem, in its strange relationship with witchcraft, empties itself of much of the grandiloquence and pomposity of romanticism. The poet, in his subtle relationship with the mystic, rids himself of the traits of the Hugoesque prophet and the vain ivory-tower attitude of a Vigny. This emphasis on the poet as the sorcerer in search of the unknown and the surreal part of his being has also caused him to give up the poetry of love, or especially the facile love poetry of a Musset. Except for the poems of Eluard, a few pages of Breton, and a few poems of Apollinaire, there has been no love poetry in France since Baudelaire!

The modern poet in France has become the magician, in accordance with the precepts of Mallarmé, or a visionary, in the tradition of Rimbaud, by his willful or involuntary exploration of dreams and subconscious states. He prefers, to the coherence and the colors of the universe celebrated by the romantics, the incoherence and the half-tones of the hidden universe of the self. There the poet has learned to come upon thoughts and images in their nascent form, in their primitive beginnings, before a conscious control has been exercised over them. The *vert paradis* of the child's world, first adumbrated by Baudelaire, is the world the modern poet has tried to rediscover. To descend into it brought about a divorce between the poet and the real world around him. The world of childhood and innocence is so obscured in mystery and has been so outdistanced by the activities of adulthood that to return there, a system of magic, a new series of talismans, has to be invented. The richest source of the poet turns out to be the subconscious, precisely that world in himself that had not been expressed. The pride of the romantic poet and the somewhat melodramatic attitude he so often created for himself unquestionably helped him later to discover new regions of his spirit. The historical period of romanticism is seen more and more clearly to have been the preparation for the richer periods of symbolism and postsymbolism, when the poetic word is understood in terms of its potential magic and the symbol in its power of exorcism.

The critical writings of Baudelaire, Mallarmé, and Valéry are as important as their poetry. They discovered, as if for the first time, some of the oldest laws of poetry. What Racine did in the seventeenth century for the ageless laws of tragedy, Baudelaire did in the nineteenth century for the ageless laws of poetry. He saw the constraints of rhythm and rhyme to be not arbitrary, but imposed by a need of the human spirit. A great line of poetry combines a sensual element with an intellectual vigor, and Valéry marveled at the delicate equilibrium that poetry established between them. This very equilibrium was defined by the modern poet as witchcraft, or the incantation of the word, which no other kind of word possesses.

Thus, poetry is not the art of obstacles and rules, but the art of triumph over obstacles and the transcending of adventure, brutality, love, and sorrow. Modern poetry will one day be described as the revindication of the profoundest principle of classicism where the most universal problems of life are transcribed in a style of language that has reached a high degree of enchantment. The most obscure mysteries of the French language, and of language in general, were explored by Rimbaud, in his seeming anarchy and disorder, and by Mallarmé, in his seeming abstractions and absences. The poetry toward which they were moving, and which they almost reached, was poetry that would have sung only of itself. Claudel and Valéry, in their time and in their acknowledged role of disciples, realized more acutely than Rimbaud and Mallarmé the perils of such an attainment, and they willfully diverted poetry from anarchy or verbal alchemy to a religious celebration of the universe, and from the dream of poetic purity to a celebration of the intellect.

Just at the moment when poetry might have become an abnegation or a defeat, Claudel redefined it as a conquest of the universe. Claudel's method, the new freedom of poetic expression developed by Léon-Paul Fargue, the new strength of poetic enumeration and breath discovered by Saint-John Perse, helped to close off the danger that poetry courted in the writings of Rimbaud and Mallarmé. If with Mallarmé poetry stopped being essentially a lofty mode of expression, it became in the subsequent poets what it had been only partially with Mallarmé—an instrument of knowledge, an art in the service of the human spirit, utilized in order to reach a higher degree of domination and knowledge of self. Cubism, surrealism, and existentialism have been some of the successive chapters in this same quest dominated by poetic experimentation.

Several French critics in the middle of the century—Rolland de Renéville, Thierry Maulnier, Jean Paulhan, Jules Monnerot, Roger Caillois, Maurice Blanchot—devoted the major part of their work to inquiries into the meaning and the scope of poetry. Their investigations and elucidations are varied, but they all agree on seeing poetry as one of the extreme "experiments" of modern times. The basis of their work is in their several interpretations of symbolism, in their effort to analyze the poet's indifference toward the world, his narcissism, and how close he came to a destruction of poetry by itself. They are the major critics who have seen the poetry of postsymbolism in France, the poetry published between 1900 and 1950, as the reconstruction of poetry.

Because of the extreme solitude of the poet, spoken of by Baudelaire and poignantly epitomized in the life stories of Rimbaud and Corbière, and because of the extreme detachment from the world exemplified in the art of Mallarmé, poetry almost ceased being the full creation that it really is. The past eighty years have witnessed a return of poetry to the joys and sufferings of man. This has signaled a revindication of the freedom of poetry, after the dizzying lessons of magic and abstractions of Rimbaud's alchemy and Mallarmé's purity. The act of constructing a poem has helped the poet to construct himself. The miracle of poetry has always been the conferring of a new life on that which already has life. By means of the word, designating signs in the physical world, the poet creates a world that is eternal. The lucidity with which the modern poet has learned to do this would probably not have developed without the examples of Baudelaire and the two major poets who succeeded him.

A poem is a marriage between expression and meaning. In order to compose the poem, the poet has to question everything all over again, because a successful poem is a new way of seeing and apprehending something that is familiar. This is Mallarmé's profoundest lesson, and it seems now to be fully incorporated in the contemporary poetic consciousness. The poet's power of questioning the universe is essential. His capacity to be amazed at what he beholds is his sign. Without it, his poem will never be the revelation it should be—the revelation to himself and to his readers of what his questioning glance has resurrected, illuminated, and understood. In order to be amazed, the poet has to practice a freedom that is unusual because it is related to everything: the physical world, morality, mythology, God. The practice of this freedom ensures what we may best call the poetic response to the world and to everything in it. This is vigilance, attentiveness, lucidity: all those disciplines that are impossible to define but that the artist needs in order to achieve his work.

Since 1940, French poetry has drawn its themes more directly from the tragic quality of contemporary events—war, catastrophe—than it did in the periods of Baudelaire and Mallarmé. And yet this newer poetry is far from being a *reportage* or direct transcription. The lesson taught by Mallarmé that there is no such thing as "immediate" poetry is to such a degree the central legacy of modern poetry that the younger poets move instinctively toward the eternal myths, like that of Orpheus, which are just beyond the event, the first reaction to it and the first sentiments.

The myth is man's triumph over matter. It is his creation of a world drawn from the world of appearance.

It is the world of poetry we are able to see and comprehend far more easily than the real world. This process was once called inspiration or enthusiasm by the Greeks. The modern poets prefer to call it the alchemy or the quintessence of the word.

French poetry is still engaged in one of the richest periods of its long history. Its roots are in symbolism, in the achievements of poetry between Baudelaire's *Les Fleurs du Mal* (1857) and the death of Mallarmé (1898). The first half of the twentieth century was dominated by four major writers, all born around 1870, and who reached the status of classical writer. Two were prose writers, Proust and Gide, and two were poets, Valéry and Claudel. Their common background was symbolism. Each reacted to symbolism in his own way and according to his own purposes. The first decade of the century was very much a part of the 1890s. These four writers had begun writing and publishing by the turn of the century, but recognition of their importance did not come until soon after World War I, about 1920.

Mallarmé was the guide, director, and high priest of symbolism. Rimbaud repudiated a literary career and had no direct influence on symbolism, although he wrote between 1869 and 1875. The example of Verlaine counted very little in the symbolist period. His was poetry of the heart and pure sentiment, a tradition maintained by Francis Jammes (1868–1938), who belonged to the first genera-tion of twentieth-century poets. Even more isolated from the central evolution of French poetry stands Charles Péguy (1873–1914), cele-brated for his deeply religious poetry on Notre Dame de Chartres and for his *Mystère de la Charité de Jeanne d'Arc* (1910).

The combined examples and influences of Mallarmé and Rim-baud have proved more permanent and vital than any other in the twentieth century. The word "purity," a concept with which modern poetry is permeated, is associated primarily with Mallarmé, with the doctrine he expounded on Tuesday evenings for so many years (1880–98) in his apartment on the rue de Rome. There his most brilliant disciple, Paul Valéry (1871–1945), in his early twenties, listened to Mallarmé's conversations on poetry. The leading sym-bols of Mallarmé's purity: his virgin princess Hérodiade, his faun, more interested in his own ecstasy than in the nymphs, his swan caught in the ice of the lake. All reappear, changed but fully recognizable in the leading symbols of Valéry's poetry: his Narcissus, the contemplation of self pushed to its mortal extreme; his Jeune Parque, and marine cemetery. *La Jeune Parque* (1914–17), composed during the war years, reflects in no way the events of the war. This poem, with the major poems of Mallarmé, with Rimbaud's *Les Illuminations*, and the early prose pieces of Gide, treated so pervasively the theme of solitude and detachment that it created a new mythology of poetic purity and human absence. This was poetry of exile, written outside the social sphere. It bore no relationship to a society or world that might have been comparable to the bond between the poetry of Racine and the monarchy of Louis XIV.

Rimbaud, in his own way, is as profound an example as Mallarmé of this separation of poetry from the immediate world. The experience of the *bateau ivre* was not only an exploration of exoticism and of the unknown, it was also a lesson on the exile that is man's solitude. After writing his poetry of exile, Rimbaud lived in exile in the deserts and cities of Abyssinia. The same need for voyage and solitude was felt by Claudel (1868–1955), who claimed Rimbaud as his master in poetry, as the writer who revealed to him the presence of the supernatural in the world. Rimbaud's ambition was to move beyond literature and poetry, and this was realized by Claudel, whose vocation as poet was always subordinated to his role of apologist of Catholicism. The form of his *verset* is reminiscent of the rhythms in *Les Illuminations* and *Une Saison en Enfer*. He continued Rimbaud's Dionysian turbulence, whereas Valéry, in his more chastened, more classical style, represented, with Mallarmé, the Apollonian tradition of French poetry.

Rimbaud's real disciples were not the symbolists of the 1880s and 1890s. They were the surrealists of 1925–35. Claudel was the first to understand and appropriate Rimbaud's lesson on poetry. His *Cinq Grandes Odes* of 1911 and his *Poèmes de guerre* of 1922 treat the universe as the communication of God to man.

The second generation of poets were those men born at the end of the century. On the whole, they participated in the experience of World War I more directly than the generation of Valéry and Claudel. In fact, some of the most gifted writers of that generation lost their lives in the war: Apollinaire, Alain-Fournier, Ernest Psichari, Charles Péguy. The poet was for them a far less exalted being than he had been for Mallarmé and Rimbaud. The intellectualism and aestheticism of the late symbolist period were drastically modified and diminished. The experience of the war and the rise of the cinema were only two of the many new forces that were shaping the younger poets at that time. *La Nouvelle Revue Française*, founded in 1905 by Jacques Copeau, André Gide, and Jean Schlumberger, became, between 1920 and 1940, an organ of great influence. It was a literary chapel, exclusive as such groups tend to be, but intelligent and judicious in its power. Its editor, Gaston Gallimard, was responsible for the publication of most of the major literary texts during that time.

The oldest figures of this second generation were Max Jacob and Léon-Paul Fargue, both born in 1896. They had begun publishing poetry long before the war, but their influence was felt after the war. Stylistic traits of Verlaine and Laforgue are as present in their writing as characteristics of Mallarmé and Rimbaud. They were both friends of painters and musicians and participated actively in the avant-garde movement in France. Jacob died in the German prison of Drancy, in 1944. Fargue survived the war and died in 1947.

Surrealism was the most significant literary movement in France between symbolism and existentialism. It flourished especially in the decade 1925–35 and attracted many of the younger poets. Pierre Reverdy, born in 1889, was as closely allied to symbolism as to surrealism. Tristan Tzara, born in Romania in 1896, was the founder of the Dada movement, in collaboration with Jean Arp and Hugo Ball, in Zurich in 1916. Dadaism was the immediate forerunner of surrealism. André Breton, the leading spirit and theorist of surrealism, born in 1896, made attempts after World War II to revive surrealism as an organized movement.

Some of the most orthodox of the surrealists died before the middle of the century: René Crevel (1900–1935), whose suicide was interpreted as an act of heroism; Robert Desnos (1900–1945), a victim of a German concentration camp; Antonin Artaud (1895–1948), who spent the last nine years of his life in an insane asylum. Louis Aragon, born in 1897, became the best-known Resistance poet, but by that time had broken all ties with surrealism. The oldest of the surrealist group, Paul Eluard, born in 1895, was one of the most gifted.

Jean Cocteau (1892–1963) wrote poetry intermittently throughout his career. He remains one of the most gifted poets of his generation, even if his signal success in other genres—theater, cinema, criticism—has somewhat detracted from his position as poet. One of the most independent modern poets, Henri Michaux (1899–1984) enlarged the domain of poetry. He was discovered in 1941 by André Gide, whose fervent criticism introduced him to a wider public than he had known. With Aragon, Jacques Prévert (1900–1977) is probably the most widely read of the French poets. More important than his poetry is his writing for films. *Les Visiteurs du Soir* and *Les Enfants du Paradis* are two major successes.

The ambition of this younger generation was, in general, to recall the poet to reality after the long experimentation of poetry with language, with the symbol, with the poet's hieratic role. The newer writers felt a greater desire for communication, for immediate communication with the reader. They appropriated the common basis of world events and world problems for their verse. This tendency had already been visible in the poetry of Eluard, of Jules Supervielle, and of Michaux.

Existentialism, as a literary movement, did not develop any poets, with the possible exception of Francis Ponge, on whose work Sartre himself wrote a long essay. Although Ponge was born in 1899, his first important publication was in 1942, *Le parti pris des choses*, a poetic work of great vigor and objectivity. In describing an object—a pebble, for example, or a piece of bread—Ponge wrote also as a moralist, as a contemporary of La Fontaine.

By many, and especially by Breton, Aimé Césaire (born in 1913) was considered the first major black poet in French. He lives in Martinique. Not until after World War II was his poetry discovered in France. Breton acclaimed him as one of the legitimate heirs of surrealism by reason of the violence and richness of his poems, and by the spirit of revolt against an unjust society.

Paul Valéry:
The Dream of Narcissus

The source and explanation of every significant poem are the entire life of the poet and his reactions to the world around him. The meaningful lines of a major poem are answers to problems that the poet has asked himself and that the world has asked him; or they are echoes of phrases often repeated by his subconscious self or persistent sentences that have guided his conscience.

The art, temperament, intellect, and struggles of Paul Valéry are all present in *Fragments du Narcisse*. Composed between 1919 and 1922 and published in *Charmes* in 1922, it is an exercise on a theme that obsessed Valéry throughout his life, both in the narrow sense of the Greek myth and in the broader philosophical sense of the "self." There is an earlier and a later text on the subject of Narcissus. *Narcisse parle*, a sonnet of 1890, went through many versions before it was published in *Album de vers anciens* in 1920. Almost at the end of his life, Valéry wrote *Cantate du Narcisse* for the composer Germaine Taillefer, in 1938. These poems, especially *Fragments du Narcisse* and the comments Valéry made on them, and his more general observations on the study of the self, form his autobiography, the kind of autobiography devoid of specific details of dates and events that he would have approved.

Between 1890 and 1891, Valéry was a law student in Montpellier. His first meetings that year with Pierre Louÿs and André Gide, which have been often described, were significant events in the history of French poetry, because the young Paris aesthetes encouraged Valéry in his love of poetry and soon introduced him to Mallarmé, who became, avowedly, his master.

Gide, in his *Nourritures Terrestres*, speaks of the Jardin des Plantes in Montpellier, where he and his friend Ambroise (Paul-Ambroise Valéry) used to walk and discuss poetry. The self, *le moi*, was a central theme in their conversation, a notion that fascinated both, and that both, in different ways, were to explore in their writings. Valéry will always be struck by the principle of the multiple uncertainties that form and inhabit the self. He will always be drawn to the dangerous beauty of self-knowledge. Knowledge is godlike and serene and stable, whereas the nature of man is always human and restless and variable.

Valéry was not only a thinker, he was also a poet and wrote extensively on poetry as a craft and a technique, on what poetic composition means, on what meaning such a word as "inspiration" has for him, on the purpose of poetry and on its limitations. He claimed that "inspiration" for a poem does not come to him from emotion, but rather from an idea that flashes through his mind spontaneously and that can be provoked by the most banal type of happening: the poet's encounter with a man carrying a ladder, or his encounter with a woman returning from the market.

In many passages of his work Valéry is a moralist, a theorist, a technician. The way in which he undertakes the writing of poetry is more difficult to understand. Landscapes, the shape and poses of the human body, the impulses of the psyche, are themes in his poems. He is constantly establishing an opposition between life and the mind of the poet observing life. Life never comes to a completion, and a poem is therefore never completed until the poet's death arrests all future work on it. Valéry was always tempted to look upon his anxiety as his real profession. Anxiety precedes the writing of a poem, and helps in the writing, and continues in every stage of the composition. "*Angoisse, mon véritable métier!*"

The personal incidents in Valéry's life are not known with any certainty. In 1892 he suffered over love for a woman, but there is no trace of this passion in his early poems. There is probably some trace of it in *Fragments du Narcisse*, in the second part of the poem, but this is so universalized and transposed that it is not the autobiography of Paul Valéry but a poet's creation. Valéry always showed scorn for this trivia in a man's life, for the incidental and the transitory. It would seem that the summer night in Genoa, in 1892, when the young poet underwent a moment of illumination, did mark a change in him and resulted in a decision to give up everything, including the writing of poetry, in order to make progress in self-knowledge (*pour l'avancement en soi-même*). He began a period of study, of self-analysis, of rigorous introspection, in order to answer the question of who he was, as well as Nietzsche's question, "What is the potential of man?"

The inner life of a man thus became a kind of spectacle he observed and in which he was the subject of the play and the actor. This is the complex triple drama of Narcissus. What began for

Valéry as an exercise in meditation and contemplation was ultimately converted into a literary work. As the method of contemplation developed and matured, so did the desire to recast what was
seen. Such a desire for a poet is his "poetics," his method of giving
reality to the creatures and creations of his mind. The composition
of the poem, which is the bringing to life of a secretive vision of the
self, forces the poet to revelations of which he may be unaware. A
self-portrait is one the author may not fully recognize but that will
reveal him to the reader or the spectator.

The poetic language used by Valéry in all the poems of *Charmes*,
where *Fragments du Narcisse* occupies a central position, is both a
purified speech from which all unnecessary elements have been
discarded, and a speech of liberation where the sentiment is allowed
to grow to its fullest intensity. In Valéry's career these poems
followed his long silence. They testify to the intellectual ambition
that was the reason for the long silence.

When, in 1912, Gide asked his friends to collect Valéry's poems
and publish them in one volume, Valéry consented and expressed
his wish to wrote one more poem to be included with the early
poems. Between 1912 and 1917, he worked on *La Jeune Parque*,
which was published separately in 1917. This "exercise," which
turned out longer than he had planned, had revived his taste for
writing poetry. *Album de vers anciens*, the collection of early pieces,
appeared in 1920. Between 1919 and 1922, Valéry wrote the poems
for which he used the general title *Charmes*, and which were published in 1922. The mysterious word *charmes*, from the Latin *carmina*,
means primarily "poems," but it also means "magic" or "enchantment." It therefore designates the primitive magical function of
speech. A poem is a "charm," an alliance of sound and meaning,
destined to bewitch the reader's senses and his mind. Valéry often
referred to the chance accidents in life that may determine a career
or a work of art.

In a corner of the Jardin des Plantes in Montpellier is an inscription: *narcissa placandis manibus* ("to appease the shade of Narcissa"),
used by Valéry as an epigraph to his early poem *Narcisse parle*. This
Narcisse was the daughter of the English poet Edward Young, who,
suffering from tuberculosis, had come to Montpellier to consult
with the eminent physicians of the medical faculty and enjoy the
sunlight of Provence. Narcissa died soon after coming to Montpellier and a gardener dug her grave in an isolated corner of the
public garden. In using this inscription for *Narcisse parle*, Valéry
deliberately confused, or fused, the sad modern story of Young's

daughter with the Greek myth of the youth who fell in love with his own reflection.

In his early years in Montpellier, Valéry associated the art and secrets of poetry with his frequent walks and meditations in the Jardin des Plantes. In one of his later texts, *Lettre de Mme Emilie Teste*, he describes a fountain in the garden, *des bassins ronds et surhaussés* (round and raised-up lakes), as that place where he understood the sentiment of solitude, where he lived hours very different from his hours of sociality. The garden with its fountain was a secret place for him where he cultivated images that seemed to belong to his inner life. Gide understood the importance of this place for Valéry and celebrated it briefly in his *Nourritures Terrestres*. In one sense, then, the source of *Fragments du Narcisse* is in a fountain of Montpellier, but in a deeper sense it is in the intense secret life of the poet, in the silence where he learned to live. Valéry, known as the antiromantic, knew all the familiar storms of passion but refused to transcribe them in his poems.

As an epigraph to *Fragments du Narcisse*, Valéry used the Latin phrase *Cur aliquid vidi?* (Why did I see something?). It is taken from Ovid's work *Tristes II*, but the story of Narcissus and the nymph Echo is related by Ovid in the third book of the *Metamorphoses*. The real subject of the Valéry poem, however, had already been used in the prose work *La Soirée avec Monsieur Teste* of 1896. It is the subject of man's conscience. The attainment to lucidity about oneself, to a full awareness of one's motives and desires, brings with it both pleasure and pain. What is seen (*Cur aliquid vidi?*) is both gratifying and terrifying. In the early *Narcisse parle*, in *Fragments du Narcisse*, and at the end of his life in *Cantate du Narcisse*, which concludes the volume *Mélanges*, Valéry uses the hero Narcissus as the adolescent in love with himself, but especially as the man engaged in self-analysis, who comes to realize the inexhaustibility, the endlessness of the self, and the complex conflicting sentiments that compose the self.

Valéry can believe only in himself. He is a unity separated from the world, who can know the world only as it is apprehended by his senses and by his mind. Beyond his physical body, his senses, and the powers of memory and reasoning of his mind, there is nothing. Such were Valéry's convictions from the beginning. In writing *La Jeune Parque* and the poems that immediately followed it, Valéry was opposing, in his style and themes, the current of poetry popular between 1918 and 1925. The intellectual rigor of Valéry's writing and the classical diction of his verse represented

the culmination of symbolist poetry. But the idols of the day—
Apollinaire, Max Jacob, Cocteau, and the surrealists Breton, Phi-
lippe Soupault, and Aragon—represented a completely different
poetic practice, at odds with Valéry's in the irrational tendencies of
their verse.

Fragments du Narcisse is a long poem on the encounter of a young
man with his own image. Whereas in the myth the beauty of his
face and body is the cause of his wonderment, in Valéry's poem the
cause of the wonderment and self-examination is more dominantly
philosophical. The erotic attraction is certainly present, but the
protagonist is struck by the contrast between his uniqueness and
his universality. In the *Cahiers*, Valéry names the two angels,
Knowledge and Eros (*Connaissance et Eros*), and these preside in
quite even power over the principal subject: the properties of
thought, its subtlety, and its even-flowing quality.

The poem is in three parts, each of which was published at
different times. The first *fragment*, and the longest, of 148 lines, is
a monologue spoken by Narcissus, who has just come to the edge
of the water. The daylight is changing into the first dark of evening.
As he sees himself in the water, he hopes the nymphs will continue
to sleep, because on awakening, they would disturb the water's
surface and dispel his image, which he wants to contemplate. But
this contemplation does not bring peace to Narcissus. He is *l'inquiet
Narcisse*, anxious and troubled. Much of the passage is on nature—
the air, the forest smells, the reflections, the setting sun—but everything brings Narcissus back to his fever, to his memories, to his
pride, and his impotency, to what he calls in the last two words of
the passage *"inépuisable Moi."*

The second *fragment*, of 116 lines, opens with an apostrophe to the
fountain. Momentarily, Narcissus interrupts his self-examination to
invoke the many dramas of love to which the fountain has been
witness. He invokes the passionate intensity of love between two
human beings, as well as the disappointments and bitterness that
destroy the passion. To the familiar story of love and its dissolution,
Narcissus opposes his own drama of solitude.

The third *fragment*, of 50 lines, resumes and terminates the monologue. In it Narcissus acknowledges the impossibility of joining
with the images he loves. He thereby underscores the great distance
between the ephemeral and the profound parts of his being. In
wishing to join with his double, Narcissus shatters the image of
love.

These are the three moments or scenes of the meditation that Valéry made into his most poignant poem on the conscience and the consciousness of the self. Implicit from the beginning, and growing in intensity throughout the poem, is the conviction that love and death are inseparable. In countless ways this duality is sung of in the poem. It is in the changing of day into night. It is in the confronting of the mind and the body, the myth of the self and its appearance. It is in the presence of Narcissus at the edge of the fountain and in the absence of Narcissus in his reflection. It is in his desire and in the impossibility of his seizing the object of his desire.

During the unfolding of the myth, Valéry describes the calm of the forest scene, the silence of the fountain, and the youth's discovery of his image. As he remains immobile, his love grows in him until it reaches a high point of fervor. As thus narrated, it is also the myth of poetry, the discovery of poetry as it rises up in the self when the self is immobilized and totally attentive to the emotion that is forming in words. The happiness of the poet is the tranquility of the self when he allows the image to form. So Narcissus and his image are in reality the poet and his poem. They are as totally separated one from the other as Narcissus is separated from his image, but they are bound to one another in the sense that one is dependent on the other, that one comes from the other.

Fragments du Narcisse is a solemn monologue. A tragedy is enacted in it, and one senses this tragedy at the beginning with the change from daylight to darkness. Night falls over the scene with the inevitability associated with tragedy. It is a sign of the presence of the gods who are in control of the fate of this youth. What is to happen will have to happen, and it will happen to every man. The law is inexorable. As Valéry faithfully rehearses the characteristics of the myth, he comes upon the many worlds contained in the myth, which are myths within the myth. The mind of Narcissus, in its tranquility, contains the world, as the waters mirror the forest. And in the world is the body of Narcissus, which alone attracts him, and in the body of Narcissus is his mind, which discovers, restores, and prolongs his desire. Why is this enacted as tragedy? Because of the ultimate discovery of introspection: that between the self that loves and the object of his love is the distance of infinity, a separation of worlds, one as far apart from the other as day is from night, as a real body is from its reflection. The inescapable tragedy is the regular rhythm of verses composed with the absolute assurance of their musical properties, of words chosen for their strength and delicacy which transcribe the emotion of the poet as he watches nature itself lead him to the heart of the ego's tragedy. The tragedy is bearable because of the poem's formality. We follow our fate because of the mind's victory in comprehending fate.

The opening line in *Fragments du Narcisse* is brilliantly conceived to demonstrate the two aspects of tragedy that will penetrate the entire poem. On the one hand, tragedy is an event that is safe and inevitable, and on the other hand, it is ambiguous because the mind refuses to believe or is unable to comprehend it. There is a finality (*enfin*) in the first line, and each word is ambiguous:

> *Que tu brilles enfin, terme pur de ma course!*

The entire phrase may be hortatory ("May you shine at last . . .") or exclamatory ("How you shine at last!). The object addressed, *tu . . . terme*, may be the literal end of the race through the forest or it may be death itself. And the adjective *pur* may refer to the limpid surface of the water as it shines (*brilles*) or it may be the absolute of death. The entire line, therefore, may be the boy's expression of pleasure at seeing the fountain, or it may be an expression of his desire to behold the shining water. Suspended and separated from the rest of the poem, the line announces both a violent action (*ma course*) and a perfected or absolute ending (*terme pur*) of the action.

Then, immediately, with the first long stanza of fifteen lines, the ambiguity vanishes and we are involved in a scene where the unnamed protagonist is compared to a deer (*cerf*) coming to the edge of the water to slake its thirst, and where the nymphs in the water are told to continue sleeping so that the surface of the water will be untroubled. We are in a world strongly reminiscent of Mallarmé's *L'Après-Midi d'un faune*, with the animal referred to, the nymphs, their sleep, and the forest setting. But whereas the faun's attraction to the nymphs was perfectly natural, here in Valéry's poem the love of the protagonist is called "curious": *cette amour curieuse*. He prays for the continuance of stillness and of the nymph's sleep, so that he can see and undergo the bewitchment:

> *Votre sommeil importe à mon enchantement.*

> (I need your sleep for my bewitchment.)

The self is mirrored and sees a face. And gradually the speech becomes more direct. The protagonist speaks of his own beauty and suffering (*ma beauté, ma douleur*). The water, where this beauty is visible, is apostrophized, both its surface and its depths. The figure is assured of his solitude. *Je suis seul!* But he knows that all about him the mysteries of the universe are attentive. He speaks of the gods and the echoes and the ripples. The atmosphere is not unlike the early scene in *Phèdre* where the suffering queen is aware of her ancestors the gods and where the silence of Trézène is only a specious silence. Tragedy begins at a great distance in time and space. The forces that plot against man are mathematically calculated in some region beyond the limits of his senses.

The stillness, as if personified, listens to the youth, and in that stillness he listens to hope. "The night air on his body seems to be telling him that he loves this body:

La nuit vient sur ma chair lui souffler que je l'aime.

In eight lines (48–55) that the poet once claimed were the most perfect he had ever written, Valéry describes the sunset. The comparison is with a woman who, after the act of love, gradually loses the high coloration of her body and goes to sleep. The sunset itself and the eroticism of the passages are both important for the following stanza (56–71), when the calm of night is total, when the tyranny of the youth's body becomes a stronger theme, and when he names himself for the first time. In leaning over the water, he sees the ruddy water subside and looks for the picture of a god. But a swan has silently moved off (could it be Jupiter?) and the naked body mirrored gives not peace to Narcissus but worry and torment:

Pour l'inquiet Narcisse, il n'est ici qu'ennui!

The seeming peace of the water makes him dizzy (*la paix vertigineuse*) because he senses the limitless depths beneath the image. He is dizzy from the vision, which is "pure" in its shimmering surface and "fatal" at the same time. The two adjectives *fatal* and *pur* describe the destiny of Narcissus, which contains the absolute and the knowledge of death.

With a change of rhythm (alexandrines alternating with octosyllabic lines), an incantation begins, addressed to the water, to the depths that contain the dreams that are looking at Narcissus. The ambiguity of the word *profondeur*, both water and the deep secrets of the self,

> *Profondeur, profondeur, songes qui me voyez*

> (Depth, depth, dreams that see me)

leads to a passage on the beauty of the body, described as the perfect prey (*cette parfaite proie*). The self, in the experience, is both seducer and prey, both admirer and victim. The beloved figure cannot be removed from his crystal world. To extract him from the water would be to destroy him.

The nymph Echo is far away from this Valéry scene. All the sounds—the wind and the birds—mingle in an auspicious way, and Narcissus feels them to be expressions of the gods speaking his secrets to the air. He is held to this one spot by eternal forces of attraction.

The dilemma grows more and more implacable as the beauty of the image becomes clearer and the desire more insistent. The figure on the water is similar to Narcissus, his double in fact, but more perfect than Narcissus and separated from him only by the night. The increasing darkness forces Narcissus to lower his head even closer to the surface. "So close that he could drink the face he watches":

> *Je suis si près de toi que je pourrais te boire,*
> *O visage . . .*

All of his senses are focused on the one sense of sight. In eight lines (136–43) the infinitive *voir* is used four times with the insistence of a prayer: to see not only the beauty of a face, but to see also the secrets contained within the forehead that is mirrored. The long *fragment* ends with five lines that recapitulate the dilemma and redefine it in the strongest terms. It begins with the first-person pronoun *Je* and ends with the pronoun turned noun: *Moi*. The duality is clear: the "I" recording the experience and the "self" that is undergoing the experience. All possible companions are rejected:

> *Nulle des nymphes, nulle amie ne m'attire.*

(No one of the nymphs, no friend attracts me.)

Solitude is necessary and august. Eroticism is indistinguishable from desire and it is inexhaustible. But this final adjective, *inépuisable*, is attached to the self (*Moi*). The self in its duality is both desire and the object of desire. The ancient myth has at this point been fully re-created by Valéry, and partially interpreted also. But the interpretation continues in the second and third fragments.

The intensity reached at the end of part I has to be relaxed. Part II is quite different. It is a necessary intervening scene when the love of man and woman is evoked in order to offset the extraordinary solipsism of the first *fragment* and create a pause before returning to the drama of self-love.

The fountain is apostrophized now, serenely and in a manner that seems detached from the fountain-mirror:

Fontaine, ma fontaine, eau froidement présente.

(Fountain, my fountain, water coldly present.)

The poet is reminded of the fountain's age, of the years that have gone by, and of all the beings that have stopped by the water's side. Nature (*roses*), time (*saisons*), and the physical experience of love (*les corps et leurs amours*) (bodies and their love) have been observed by the water. It is the witness to all of life. It has witnessed the greatest characteristic of life, that characteristic that gives to men their deepest desolation and anguish: the passing of life, the changes, and the disintegration. This applies even to the greatest of human experiences, to love itself:

L'amour passe et périt.

(Love passes and dies.)

The generality is first stated, and then the fragment is given over to an analysis of love. Verses 171–91 form a passage of dense sensuality where the violence, the imperiousness of sexual love, is described. The joining of male and female makes one "monster" (a famous line in *Othello* at the beginning of the play comes to mind), after the caresses, the mounting of the blood, the lust, the kisses, the moaning, and the momentous climax. But the monster, once formed, died. Physical love is a momentary exaltation. The fountain had watched it grow and dissolve countless times. The reeds around the fountain have heard the sighs of lovers year after year. The memories of happiness and unhappiness in love are attached to every spot in nature around the fountain: the cypress tree, the rose, the place where the sea air was strong.

Before speaking again of himself, Narcissus—because the entire poem is a soliloquy—in a hard-wrought stanza (211–30) speaks of the bitterness that follows love, of the emptiness that succeeds exaltation, of the very paths in the forest that finally become for the lovers a labyrinth where the Minotaur lives and curses the sun.

This passage on the separation from the intensity of love leads Narcissus back to himself, to his own form of love, which from this point on in the meditation becomes more philosophical. The youth is curious only about his own essence:

> *Mais moi, Narcisse aimé, je ne suis curieux*
> *Que de ma seule essence.*

The new tone of peaceful introspection (231ff.) contrasts with the erotic and hopeless violence of the preceding passages. How can the most handsome of mortals love anyone else save himself? He has accepted the concept of his solitude, of the one body that he possesses and that is his own:

> *cher corps, je n'ai que toi!*

He welcomes the infinite exchange between himself and his image that the faint light from the moon permits. The important words are *un échange infini*: an exchange that can go on for as long as there is visibility. Exchange and not union. The boy he watches is of the water and of himself. He knows now that this other half of him is only light.

But such pure contemplation is exasperating. Narcissus wants the perils of lovemaking: the hands that join, the violence, the sobbings. He wants the silence to come to an end and hear words spoken by this inaccessible cruel youth depicted on the water with his grace and virility.

The relatively brief third fragment (265–314) recasts this violence with a series of questions to which the answers will be the final formulation of tragedy. The fountain is now called an abyss and the reflected image is the inhabitant of the abyss, the "specious host" of the sky who has been hurled down from the heavens. In the words *hôte spécieux*, we read both the beauty of the image and the deception this beauty brings. The water's surface is likened to a dark sky because it bears a relationship with the heavens of the gods, who have determined the fate of the protagonist. The full truth, thanks to these symbols, is going to emerge now. Narcissus has already acknowledged that the body he desires is a mere reflection on the surface of a deep fountain. He is about to learn that the real body that casts the reflection is similarly an abyss, bottomless, endless. Can it be that he too is but the reflection of a reflection?

The initial questions of this fragment conclude with the most significant of all. Who can love anything else save himself?

> . . . *Et qui donc peut aimer autre chose*
> *Que soi-même?*

In reaffirming his love for his own body, Narcissus goes one step farther, which announces the poem's conclusion. He realizes now that his body is the one object that protects him against joining the company of the dead.

> *Je t'aime, unique objet qui me défends des morts!*

This line breaks off the meditation, and when it resumes, after a pause, the tone is more quiet, more resigned. The words are now a prayer addressed to the gods, whose presiding presence we have felt from the beginning and who have been touched by this spectacle of so much love.

In one extraordinarily succinct phrase, *Pères des justes fraudes*, these gods are called "fathers of justified deceptions," because they have allowed the faint illumination of night to show to Narcissus a figure toward which he is attracted, and they have allowed him to experience the torment of love and its impossibility. The entire action of the poem is recapitulated in the two words *justes fraudes*, the deceptiveness of light and love.

The new closeness to the gods Narcissus finds permits him to utter for the last time his prayer that they arrest time and the change of light. His fate is immobility and adoration, provided that he bend down over the fountain. His torso has the smoothness of a stone, the stone of a temple where he lives. His body is the temple separating him from his divinity. Narcissus's concentration is now on his mouth, and with the word "kiss" (*baiser*), he invokes the verb "shatter" (*briser*), close in sound and dramatically close in meaning. The distance between the lips of Narcissus and the lips he yearns to kiss is almost nothing, but it is also everything; it is the distance between himself and the water, between his soul and the gods, between life and death. The consummation of love is death.

Even as this thought is articulated, the darkness of the forest deepens, and Narcissus knows that soon he will not see the beloved image. The death of the soul will be the joining with the dark, when nothing will exist between death and the self. There is no time left save that for the final act: the joining of Narcissus with his image by means of a kiss. He lowers his head, and with the fatal kiss the water is shattered. Narcissus is shattered and love takes flight:

> *L'insaisissable amour*
> *dans un frisson, brise Narcisse, et fuit . . .*

The final word *fuit*, which designates the collapse of self-love and death, is an echo of the first two lines of the poem: the *course*, the race through the forest, *la fuite*, the flight of the boy to the fountain's edge in the forest.

Nothing remains at the end. The verb *briser* makes of the water a crystal, a mirror that is shattered.

What is, in its general lines, this tragedy? What is, in its contained meditative form, this violence?

Each of the three *fragments* begins with an invocation, and what is invoked becomes the central part of the development.

I. As soon as he is at the edge of the water, Narcissus invokes the nymphs who live in the water and urges them to continue sleeping:

> *Nymphes! si vous m'aimez, il faut toujours dormir!*

(Nymphs! if you love me, you must sleep forever!)

Their sleep will assure the stillness of the water, on whose surface Narcissus will behold his image. Sight is all important for the desired experience of love, and that is why so much of this opening poem is concerned with the sunset and the coming of night. The sky, changing from a violent color to a subdued color and then to the first phases of night, is a symbol for the ecstasy of passion and the appeasement of passion. For Narcissus, it will be this experience reversed. He will first attentively, prayerfully, study his features in the water, his form, his mouth, and then the incitement to know the body will grow throughout the rest of the poem.

II. Placed between the two poems on the solitude of Narcissus, the second fragment, with its invocation to the fountain, accentuates first the distance that separates him from the water's surface, from the object of his desire. His sensibility gives over to a mental activity as he remembers the lovers who must have stopped by the fountain and experienced on this spot the closeness of their love. His mind carries him even beyond, to the disappointment and bitterness that can follow love.

III. The first word of the third fragment, *Ce corps*, is the invocation. Love, in its purely physical insistence, dominates the poem now. The body is desired, but it is impossible to embrace this body. The end of the poem is the effort to join by a kiss the real body and its image. The union takes place in death.

Thus the cycle is completed. The poem moves from daylight to night and back again to the light of self-knowledge and experience. It moves from elation to despair and back again to that elation which is the absolute of tragedy. It moves from the love of self to the love of two beings and back to solitude, and to death in solitude. The gods of tragedy are there in the fatal calm of the forest scene. Through them the violent feelings of Narcissus are foreseen and controlled. Man's fate is implacable.

No thinker has considered our age with greater perspicacity and penetration than Paul Valéry. And no thinker has demolished it more totally. The method of Valéry that has exposed so succinctly all the forces and ideas constituting a threat to civilization as we know it has been called in France a "temptation."

Valéry announced the death of civilization, and in that sense he belongs to the future. His fame has been built upon fragments: poems, aphorisms, dialogues, brief essays. The actual "subjects" of his pages are varied: the beauty of a shell, the prose of Bossuet, the method of Stendhal, the myth of Narcissus. The value of each of the pages is Valéry's own presence within the subject, the degree of conscience and consciousness with which he considers each subject.

With each essay, with each fragment of prose writing and each poem, Valéry extended the hegemony of his thought over most of the intellectual problems facing man today. Our entire historical period is in his work: the gravest problems that worry us and the oldest myths that enchant us.

Paul Claudel:
The Spiritual Quest

Paul Claudel still occupies a place in literature and in Catholic thought that is vigorously disputed. In his mid-eighties at the time of his death, in February 1955, Claudel maintained not only his full powers as a writer but his violent temper as well, and his animosities. His detractors are legion. But his admirers come from many varying beliefs, religious and political and aesthetic. He has received homage from such writers as the Catholic academician Louis Gillet and the Communist Louis Aragon, from the Protestant Charles-Ferdinand Ramuz and the humanist Jean Prévost, from Alain and Maurice Blanchot.

Claudel was born in 1868, in Villeneuve-sur-Fère, a small village in Le Tardenois, a region that lies between the provinces of Ile-de-France and Champagne. As a child he learned to observe all the details of the countryside. He has written of the natural spectacles he watched from the highest fork of an old tree he used to climb. This was the site of his first dialogues with nature, from which he drew throughout his life. The lycée in Paris, Louis-le-Grand, was for young Claudel a prison, a stifling atmosphere he has described in *Ma Conversion*.

Those were the years when, in company with other young intellectuals, Claudel read Baudelaire and Verlaine. But his first great revelation, of both a literary and spiritual order, was Rimbaud. He has described the seminal and paternal action the reading of *Les Illuminations* had on him. He first came upon some of the prose poems in the June 1886 issue of *La Vogue*. This reading constituted for him a release from what he called the hideous world of Taine, Renan, and the other Molochs of the nineteenth century. *J'avais la révélation du surnaturel* (I had the revelation of the supernatural), he wrote to Jacques Rivière. Rimbaud was the human means for Claudel's return to his faith. Certain sentences in *Une Saison en Enfer*, such as *Nous ne sommes pas au monde* (We are not in the world), never ceased to reveal to Claudel the real significance of his own revolt. Claudel was, not unlike Rimbaud, a revolutionary, a Dionysian ecstatic.

The poet has recorded that in the same year, 1886, a second event befell him that was to fix his destiny. On Christmas day, in Notre-Dame, during the service of Vespers, he experienced a spiritual awakening that was never to be impaired or endangered thereafter. In describing this conversion, Claudel speaks of its suddenness and of the perception he felt of Divine Innocence. This mystical experience was followed by four years of bewilderment and struggle to harmonize the new force in him with his former self. He began to study the Bible, the history of the Church and its liturgy, and discovered that what he had once studied as poetry was indissolubly associated with religion. He frequently attended Mallarmé's Tuesday evening gatherings and learned from the master of symbolism how to look at the universe as if it were a text to be deciphered. In his later, somewhat severe article on Mallarmé, *La Catastrophe d'Igitur*, Claudel demonstrated his debt to the older poet, although he grouped Mallarmé with Poe and Baudelaire as poets of the "metaphysical night" of the nineteenth century, who lacked an indispensable key to their art.

In China, where he went in 1895, at the beginning of a long diplomatic career, Claudel entered upon a period of solitude, silence, and meditation. His studies centered on the Bible and Saint Thomas Aquinas. To Rimbaud's doctrine on the power of poetic language, and to Mallarmé's doctrine on the symbolism of the universe, Claudel added the gigantic synthesis of Saint Thomas and the religious interpretations of metaphorical language.

By his strength, by the proportions of his work, by his attitude toward the Creation, Claudel towered above his contemporaries. By remaining outside all literary coteries, his presence was felt as a force isolated and unique. Every object in his writing is stated in terms of its meaning, of its role.

In his doctrine on the poetic word which transmits an image of the relationship of things, Claudel's debt to Rimbaud is obvious. The world is limitless in its relationships, and the poet, in his role of conqueror of the poetic word, becomes reader of the world and decipherer of its relationships.

Claudel had always claimed that Rimbaud had been one of those explorers of the nineteenth century consecrated to learning something about what creation is, what it signifies. The basis of symbolism is a belief that each thing in the world has a meaning that will be revealed to the poet who is able to understand it.

Many of the most serious of the twentieth-century artists have provided their works with an aesthetic justification. In painting, for

example, Braque has made theoretical pronouncements of consider-
able importance. Others, while not contributing any writing as
massive as Delacroix's *Journal*, have spoken at times with conviction
and acumen: Picasso, Matisse, Rouault, Masson, Severini. In literature, the achievement of Marcel Proust is the masterful way in
which he combined his novel with the analysis of its origin and its
meaning. Joyce, Mann, Gide, and Valéry have all striven to propose
a work and, at the same time, the aesthetics of the work.

The five great odes of Claudel (*Cinq Grandes Odes*) open with one
entitled *Les Muses*, inspired by a frieze of the nine muses the poet
had seen sculptured on a sarcophagus. The ode is a kind of poetics
dealing with the poetic art, with its birth and its function.

On many points the theories of Claudel converge with those of
Proust, and behind him with the tenets of impressionism and the
theories of Ruskin. These artists and theorists believe that each time
a new original artist arises the world is re-created. He is able to
confer immortality on what has no duration, a man's perception of
the world. Aesthetic truth is not the same as scientific truth. It is
based on direct observation and exact notation. The reality of the
world for an artist is his vision of the world. It is a particular universe
not seen by others until it is put in the form of art. Each work will
create its own posterity, and finally that work will reveal the temper
and soul of the period in which it was created.

In the making of the poet's metaphor or the painter's metamorphosis, the artist changes the names of things and the forms of
things in order to establish a greater contact with them, a purer
contact of intimacy. The modern artist, whether he be Claudel or
Proust, Rouault or Picabia, is greatly concerned with the relation
existing between the re-creation of art and the reality of the world.
Metaphor and metamorphosis are signs of the sovereign freedom
of man's mind to substitute one element for another, to substitute
what we usually call reality for its spiritual state.

Claudel's parable on Animus and Anima may have been written
to explain the lesson of analogy. It is the marriage of the mind and
the soul. Anima brought a good dowry to her husband, Animus.
But he is difficult in his vanity and tyrannical ways. He has numerous bad traits. He is unfaithful. He spends his time in cafés as she
cooks. One day, by chance, he hears her sing. An unusual and
wonderful song. He pleads with her to sing it again, but she refuses.
He pretends to leave the house but hides behind the door. Then he
hears her sing again and realizes the song is addressed to his wife's

Divine Lover. Animus is the part of us that divides and separates and analyzes. Anima is the part that unites and makes us one.

Her song is the poetic word that Rimbaud had talked about: a veritable instrument of discerning for the creation of a new being. The poet becomes a medium and poetry a magical means of seizing the ineffable. Claudel had before him the example of Rimbaud, and especially of Rimbaud's poetic failure.

This celebrated pair, Animus and Anima (or Eros and Agape), appears under many names. The Jungian psychoanalyst defines anima as the center of the irrational and the unconscious, the abode of the dark passions and instincts, the archetypes of both aggressive and seductive forces. Anima, on the conscious level, when freed from the control of reason, is usually referred to as a force in romanticism.

The appearance of Claudel's poetry in the twentieth century is not unlike the appearance of the Gothic cathedral in the thirteenth century. They are comparable in their depiction of the ever-dying and ever-renascent forms of the world. In them, symbolism and theology are bound with life.

Perhaps the greatest lesson Claudel has bequeathed to our age is the belief that the truth of art always tends naturally toward the sacred. The chapel of Matisse at Vence, in southern France, may justify such a term as "renascence of sacred art." The conversation between the aged bishop of Nice and the aged painter, who was not a practicing Catholic, revealed a similarity of inner spiritual life between the priest and the creative artist. The synthesis of art and faith that was so remarkable in the Middle Ages, and that may be reappearing, depends upon the inner life of man, on a certain quality of his soul, on silence, poverty, solitude, nobility. The sanctuaries recently erected at Assy, Audincourt, and Vence appear as original and new as the odes of Claudel when they were first published, and as the clowns and Christs in the paintings of Rouault.

The relationship of the poet to his poem is comparable to the relationship of God to his universe. The basic assumption in Claudel's aesthetics is the universe seen as the mirror of God, and man as the mirror of the universe. It is not difficult to move from this point to the belief that the revelation of the meaning of the world that the poet gives is expressed in the arrangement of words. The poem is not the abstract essence that may be derived from the words. The poem is the concrete reality of the arrangement of the words. The new meaning of the world lies precisely in the specific creation of the poet, which is his arrangement of words.

Here the parable of Animus and Anima seems to apply to the poet's re-creation of the world. The surface self, the animus, is constantly composing words into clear, simple, intelligible notions. But these are not the words of the poet. His words are those spoken by Anima, from the deepest part of her being. They are obscure to the poet himself until they are uttered. They are characterized by a greater totality, a greater wholeness than the words of ordinary speech.

Saint-John Perse:
The Poet's Sense of History

With the announcement in the late fall of 1960 that Saint-John Perse had been awarded the Nobel prize for literature, the work of a relatively obscure poet became a public concern. The work itself had been previously scrutinized only by that small public devoted to the cause of poetry. To a wider public now the name Saint-John Perse was known, as were the few biographical details that had often appeared in print: the birth of Alexis Saint-Léger Léger on a coral island near Guadeloupe (Saint-Léger-les-Feuilles), his education in France, his entrance into the diplomatic service in 1914, his seven-year sojourn in China, his high post at the Quai d'Orsay in the Ministry of Foreign Affairs, his refusal to work for the Vichy government, and his arrival in the United States in 1940, where he lived in Washington for seventeen years before returning to France.

Eloges (Praises), his earliest poems, was first published in 1911, with the signature Saint-Léger Léger. The new edition of 1925 appeared with the mysterious signature Saint-John Perse. The poems in *Eloges* are evocative of a childhood spent in the midst of exotic vegetation, in a harbor cluttered with colonial merchandise. The vision of the sea dominates this childhood, with its memories of cyclones, plantations, volcanoes, tidal waves.

Anabase, first published in Paris in 1924, preserves the memory of the years Léger spent in China and the Gobi Desert. This work, translated by T. S. Eliot in 1930, is one of the key poems of our age. It represents the poet as conqueror of the world, in the guise of a literal conqueror associated with arms and horses, with a willed exile in foreign places. As soon as the plans of the future city are drawn up, the conqueror leaves. Experiences and joys are enumerated, but there is always more to see and to hear. But the literal conquest related is not so important as the actual conquest of language carried out by the poet in the writing of his poem. The primitive meaning of words is fought over and won. The history of the poet is the history of man seeking possession of the entire earth.

In March 1942, *Poetry* magazine (of Chicago) published the original French text of Léger's poem *Exil*. This is much more than a poem on the war and on Perse's exile. It is on the same theme as *Anabase*, the poet's exile, the necessary "absence" that precedes every work of art: *un grand poème né de rien* (a great poem born from nothing). This concept, traditionally associated with Mallarmé, is explored and revitalized in *Exil*. Isolated from the rest of the long poem, the final line is both the summation of the work and the announcement of the poem to come:

> *Et c'est l'heure, ô Poète, de décliner ton nom,*
> *ta naissance et ta race.*

> (And the time is come, O Poet, to declare your name, your birth, and your race.)*

The sensations that come to him from the ruins, from the snows, the winds, and the sea, are each in turn to be the subject of the new poems. The form of these poems is nontraditional. Léger has perfected a broad stanza containing its own beat and pulsation. He observes the world and spells it out in his verse as it comes to him in his meditation. His speech is breath and concrete words. He enumerates all parts of the familiar world surrounding man: animals and plants and the elements, and he does not hesitate to use precise technical terms. The poem is ceremonial, involving all the diverse activities of man and stating them in successive gestures. Whatever legendary elements remain are actualized in this poetry, which is always praise, as the title of the first volume, *Eloges*, revealed.

Every critic who has written on Perse has been struck by the opulence of his words, by their solemnity, by his persistent use of *grand* and *grandeur*, of *haut* and *hauteur*, of *vaste*, and other such words that provide his work with cosmic dimensions. The figure of the Prince is associated with the themes of power and exile and language. The Prince in his world is the prototype of the poet in his poem. The Prince lives in power and impoverishment, in adornment and nudity; the poet lives in silence and language, in magic and mysticism.

Saint-John Perse was heir to one of the richest poetic traditions. The form of his poetry, as well as the metaphysical use he puts it to, recalls the examples of Rimbaud in *Les Illuminations* and of Claudel in *Cinq Grandes Odes*. He was the contemporary poet who

*Translation by Denis Devlin.

perhaps came closest to considering himself the instrument of superior revelation. When he spoke as a poet, something was affirmed in him. He knew that the most simple object or the most trite event is capable of giving birth to a poem.

Perse was obsessed and martyred by his vision, as Mallarmé and Rimbaud had been by theirs. The poet's vocation is his drama. To transcend one's existence by participating in it more profoundly is the poet's honor and suffering, whether it be Besançon or Aden or Washington. The poet's exile is his solitude and his ethics.

Language itself may be for man his deepest spiritual experience. Beyond language extends the void, the unmeasured spaces inhabited by the winds, of which Perse speaks in his poem *Vents*, the winds that blow over the face of the earth and disturb all perishable things. The opening words speak of the winds in quest of oracles and maxims, and of the narrator who seeks the favor of a god for his poem.

As much as any man of any period, Alexis Léger had traveled along the highways of many lands and across the oceans of the world. The course of his poem *Vents* expresses the meaning of such travels, the new style of grandeur he refers to, and the pure song about which there is no real knowledge. The weight of the words would seem to be the only force not dispersed by the winds. The words, riveted to the pages, are those signs, fixed forever, of things that move with the wind and die in it. "Ashes and scales of the spirit," he says, "all that taste of asylum and casbah."*

> . . . *cendres et squames de l'esprit.*
> . . . *Ha! tout ce goût d'asile et de casbah.*

Claudel, in his essay on *Vents*, published first in *La Revue de Paris* of November 1949, says that the second part of the poem evokes America, both the puritan melancholy of the North and the stagnant stupor of the South. Certain words in the text justify this claim: Audubon, sumac, hanging moss, Columbus. The poem unfolds in wave after wave of images. Their forms do not in the least appear contestable or corroded, and yet they proclaim the primacy of the obscure, the sulfurous, the pythic. The winds in this section of the poem carry with them the smell of fire.

*Translation by Hugh Chisholm.

Perse's *Vents*, as well as Rimbaud's *Une Saison en Enfer* and Baude-laire's *Les Fleurs du Mal*, are among those modern works of poetry reflecting the complex degree of sensibility that man reached in the nineteenth century and continues to maintain in the twentieth. Perse has indeed taken his place beside the four poets of modern France: Baudelaire, Mallarmé, Rimbaud, and Valéry.

The third section of *Vents* evokes the history of the conquerors, their long itineraries, the new lands, the setting up of new trade. The poet, too, belongs to the race of discoverers: to the *conquistado-res*, well diggers, astrologers. In his acquisitions he seizes with similar boldness the goals of his search, of his humor and of his sorrow. Into a poem he puts the originality of his discovery as one puts the essence of flowers into a flask.

The wind is the element giving us life. It is in our lungs and in our mouth in capsules of emptiness, necessary for us whether we move over distances covered by a Drake or a crusader, or whether we remain in one corner of the planet and perish through excess of wisdom. Poems, in a destiny comparable to the winds, bear seed and fruit. A book is a series of separations, departures, returns, of changings of speed. The fourth section of *Vents* evokes not only the plateaus of the world and the aging roads of pilgrimages. It evokes also the dilemma of man's ceaseless questioning and the equivocal mask of art placed over all interrogations.

In his last poems, *Amers* (*Seamarks*) of 1957 and *Oiseaux* (*Birds*) of 1963, Perse continued to describe and analyze the condition of man in our time, the fate of man at this moment in history. The poet's work relates the secular and spiritual efforts of man to see himself as part of the natural world, to tame the hostile powers of the world, to worship the endlessly renewed beauty of the world, to conjugate his ambitions and dreams with the changes and modifications of time. This became clear in Perse's long work *Amers*, a massive ceremonial poem.

Amers is a poem that moves far beyond the violence of man's history in order to exalt the drama of his fate, which is looked upon as a *march*, the march of all humanity. The poet himself, in a brief statement about his poem, calls it the march toward the sea, *la marche vers la mer*. The word *sea* (*la mer*) is in the title, *Amers* (*sea-marks*), those signs on the land, both natural (cliffs) and man-made (steeples), that guide navigators as they approach the shore.

The sea in the poem is both the real sea and a symbol. It is real as the source of life and it is symbolic as being the mirror reflecting the destiny of man. The march toward the sea is an image for the quest, for man's eternal search for some experience with the absolute. The search, as it continues in *Amers*, is exaltation. Man is exalted in his vocation of power and in his desire to know the absolute, to approach the divine. The image of power comes to him from the sea, and from the endless power of words. Covered with foam, the sea resembles a prophetess speaking the most sacred, the most enigmatic words of the poet:

> *La Mer elle-même tout écume, comme Sibylle en fleurs*
> *sur sa chaise de fer . . .*

(The sea itself all foam, like a sibyl in flower on her iron chair . . .)

In *Anabase* man confronts the burning of the desert sand; in *Vents* he confronts the violence of the winds, as he confronts the violence of the sea in *Amers*. Not only in *Eloges* but in all the subsequent poems, Perse praises the sky and the sea, the earth and the winds, the snow and the rains.

In his speech in Stockholm on the occasion of the Nobel prize presentations, Saint-John Perse emphasized the power of the adventure called poetry and claimed it is not inferior to the great dramatic adventures of science. The poet's purpose is to consecrate the alliance between man and the creation, and he needs the seamarks (*les amers*) to show that the alliance takes place when the land recognizes its relationship of vassal to the sea.

The sea was important in the medieval voyage of Tristan and the quest voyage for the Holy Grail. Many French poets of the nineteenth and twentieth centuries had sung of the sea: Victor Hugo in *Oceano Nox*; Baudelaire, whose *Voyage* alludes to the adventure of Ulysses and the voyage taken by the child's imagination as he pores over maps and prints; and Rimbaud, whose *Bateau Ivre* is an answer to Baudelaire's question, *Dites, qu'avez-vous vu?"* (What did you see?); Corbiére, the Breton poet, inspired by the sea and who chose the name of Tristan for himself; Valéry, the Mediterranean poet who found in the sea, contemplated from his cemetery at Sète, an incitement to life; Claudel, who, like Saint-John Perse, frequently crossed the oceans of the world on diplomatic missions, and who analyzed the religious meaning of water in his ode *L'Esprit et l'eau* (The Spirit and the Water).

In *Amers*, the sea is celebrated as that place of meeting where all the paths taken by men in every age will converge. It is the one image and the one reality able to sustain all the themes and unite them: the reality of the sea, the limitless power of life that is best transcribed by the sea, the eternity of man in his continuous action, the personal themes of man's solitude and freedom and love, and finally the poet's creation—the image of the poem.

In the love song of *Amers*, called *Strophe* (*Etroits sont les vaisseaux*) (*Narrow Are the Vessels*), the most personal, the most intimate experience of man's nature is related in terms of the sea. The beloved, when she speaks, identifies herself with the sea. She is both woman and sea, and the night of love is a sea night. During the violence of passion, the poet, in the power of his language, is re-creating the sea and re-creating his lover. From the beginning to the end of *Amers*, the sea is the sign of the poet's irrepressible need to create.

René Char:
The Poet's Vocation

René Char was born in 1907 in Vaucluse, a section of Provence. Until his recent death, he lived in a town near Avignon, Isle-sur-Sorgue. The Sorgue River starts at the fountain of Vaucluse (once immortalized by Petrarch) and flows into the Rhône. The world of Char's poetry is rural and Mediterranean. All the familiar elements of his native province are in it: crickets and almond trees, olives, grapes, figs, oranges, grass, branches of mimosa. The frequently recurring name of Heraclitus helps to fuse the Greek spirit with the Provençal. The country he describes is sun-flooded, a kingdom of space and dazzling light. Char's love of the land and his solicitude for living, growing things are the traits of the peasant in him. His manner of considering the objects of his landscape, of undertaking the hardest tasks and facing the gravest risks might also be traced to his peasant background, or, more simply, be explained by the deep sense of fraternity that characterizes Char's love of man and the soil. Like many lovers of the land, he has often shown hostility toward modern mechanization and modern forms of exploitation.

Char has never written in any of the usual ways about his understanding of the poet's vocation. But it became more and more clear, as his work continued to grow, and as the significance of his work continued to deepen, that the particular calling of the poet is his major theme. The poet's life unfolds within the limitations of man's mortal nature. Mortality and poetry are so conjugated in the writings of Char that one provides the setting for the other, that one is finally indistinguishable from the other. Char has moved away from the esoteric place assigned to the poet by Mallarmé in order to stand today in the humanistic center of his close friend Albert Camus (1913–60). The familiar picture of Char as Resistance leader, with his companions in the maquis of the Basses Alpes, in Céreste, is still remembered as we read his poetry, not only *Feuillets d'Hypnos* (*Leaves of Hypnos*), composed during the Occupation years, but the subsequent volumes as well, such as *Les Compagnons dans le jardin* (*Companions in the Garden*), of 1957.

Does this mean that Char's poetry is an example of "engaged" literature, as once advocated by Sartre? Not, certainly, in any literal sense. Poetry, according to Char, does not seem to be committed to any cause unless one calls life itself a cause and a reason for commitment. Poetry is not in the service of an idea or a party or a movement. In France today, in all countries for that matter, in the midst of overwhelming problems and insurmountable obstacles, the voice of the poet is heard as one of the few voices left, faithful to the truth that man represents and seeks, to the continuing mysteriousness of his dignity, to the belief that man's noblest efforts are salutary for himself and for humanity.

Char's verses, the aphorisms that abound in his work, and the brief, condensed tales that appear in company with the aphorisms, all speak of the nature of poetry. It is that which is lived, experienced with the penetrating realization of submitting to human destiny. It is a comparatively easy matter to describe a literary work that is about life. But such a definition would not apply to the poetry of Char. This poet looks upon his art as an assault on life and an embracing, an animation, of life. He answers, in the writing of his poems, not some outside command but the vibrancy of his nature and his feelings. No cause that can be defined as such will move him as much as the proportions of his own human nature, with its contradictions and its puzzling enigmas.

The word "risk," for example, applies to Char's conception of life as well as to his conception of poetry. The outside world in which he lives, almost as a poacher lives invading someone else's forest, is the natural world of constant change, a flowing river of things such as his favorite philosopher, Heraclitus, has described. But this is the site of risks and provocations. The things he sees there are not poems, but they discover their reality in poems. The poetic act is a finding of a form for things that otherwise would never emerge from their abyss or their silence or their possibility. It is difficult for Char to elaborate on the principles of poetry because for him poetics and poetry are hardly separable. It is unusual for a French poet not to bequeath texts on poetics and technique. Char's answer is his entire existence as a poet. The poet, he would say, has no other place to be except within poetry. The risk of poetry is precisely this responsibility of the poet in the action of drawing poetry from the poet's sleep and from his subconscious.

The risk of poetic creation is admirably transcribed in the striking antithesis of so many of Char's poems. Those poems, published in 1955, *Poèmes des deux années 1953–54*, contain examples of the contrast that Char establishes between solidity and fragility, between a sense of security and a premonition of the evanescence of things.

The titles of two of the poems are themselves antitheses: *La chambre dans l'espace* (*The Room in Space*), and *Le Rempart des brindilles* (*Rampart of Twigs*). The second poem begins in the form of a definition of the function of poetry, but the definition is so highly charged with antithesis that it is the poem. The two words "rampart" and "twigs" establish the fundamental antithesis between the world and poetry, between the fragile and the everlasting, between the mortal and the immortal.

The purity and the conciseness of Char's language make it appear primitively faithful to his reaction, to his first responses. He has sustained in his style, which is devoid of the usual poetic rhetoric, something of the secret meaning of his reactions. One remembers easily that Char's first allegiance was to surrealism. And yet in this will to record and explain his reaction to the world and to human experience, he places himself centrally within the tradition of French moralists. Char the poet and Char the moralist both denounce the vanity of life. Poetry is both a critique of poetry and a critique of illusion. Char's poems, like aphorisms, are brief and elliptical. The white space around them, like the silences that precede and follow speech, has its own message and its own suggestiveness.

If what Char writes contains both fury and tragedy, the poet is struck by the silence of the ink on the page. The oxymoron is there at the start: in the silence of the hieroglyphic characters and in the rage of the sentiments expressed. The poet is "within a curse," Char writes, in *Recherche de la base et du sommet* (*Search for the Base and the Summit*): "Il est dans la malédiction." He could not exist if he were not in accord with some mysterious law of apprehension. There is a price to pay for feeling deeply and for writing as a poet. That price is the daily assumption of peril. The ordinary man is able to fix the source of evil in the world: he traces it back to some event or cause. The poet knows that evil comes from farther back than he can remember.

The strong stylistic and moralist claims made by this new poet designate him as the heir of both symbolism and surrealism. He is a symbolist in the distance he knows exists between the occurrence of an event and its narration. He speaks of the enigmas of poetry as often as Mallarmé did, and he defines "the action of the poet as the result of these enigmas."

> *Les actions du poète ne sont que la conséquence*
> *des énigmes de la poésie.*
> > *A une sérénité crispée*

Mallarmé would call the poet a creator of enigmas. Char would agree with Mallarmé in calling a poem a quintessence, but in the straining of Char's language, in the tension of each poem and each aphoristic utterance, he defines the natural movement of poetry as a revolt.

In the tributes to his friends, René Crevel and Paul Eluard, Char exalts human life in all the attacks man has waged against injustice and deception, in man's love of the sun, and simply, in the power he feels in accomplishing an action. Some of the humanistic definitions of man, found in *Les Compagnons dans le jardin*, complete earlier definitions. He sees man's place as a coalition. "He is a flower held down by the earth, cursed by the stars because he is unable to rise to them, and solicited by death, which is his constant fate."

> *L'homme n'est qu'une fleur de l'air tenue par la terre,*
> *maudite par les astres, respirée par la mort, le souffle*
> *et l'ombre de cette coalition, certaines fois, le surélèvent.*

Here again is the prevailing paradox of Char's work: man seen as tenderness in the surge of his spirit and as an apocalyptic figure at his end. The pessimism of Heraclitus was not difficult to discover in the early work *Feuillets d'Hypnos*. The myth of tragedy is man's principal heritage, but it may accompany a lifetime of revolt against this fate.

This revolt is the subject matter of some of the greatest prose writers of modern France: Malraux, Saint-Exupéry, Camus. It is not only the subject matter of Char's poetry, it is the poetry itself. The poetry is his life lived as a maquis fighter and as a disciple of the philosopher of Ephesus. Char can no more cut himself off from the action of men, from cohabitation with men, than he can cease meditating on the tragedy of man's fate in a world of change and flux.

Char's fertile vision of the world in which he lives, of the world where all men live, is often cast into the abstract terms of a poet-philosopher. He calls it, in one passage, "that which is inconceivable." But it is also that which has "luminous points of reference, dazzling signs."

> *Nous sommes dans l'inconcevable, mais avec des repères*
> *éblouissants.*
>
> Recherche de la Base et du sommet

Thus, in a single line, which is a poem by virtue of its image and power, the world of tragedy is juxtaposed with the burning revolt of man's spirit living that tragedy. The violent contrast is at times softened: "In the gardens of men the future forests exist."

> *Dans nos jardins se préparent des forêts*
> *Les Compagnons dans le jardin*

"In the survival of man there is visible a better survival."

> *O survie encore, toujours meilleure.*
> *Les Compagnons dans le jardin*

The walker, the man who is bound to the earth and who walks on its surface, is granted some knowledge of the secret existence of things, secrets of the wind, of trees, of water. At moments in history when total destruction seems inevitable, man is unable to believe that the world, which has always been redeemed in the past, is facing its death in the very presence of man. In the future, Char may be looked upon as the apocalyptic poet of our day, as the poet who is the most persistently oppressed by the Apocalypse aspect of the mid-century and the post-mid-century.

The thought of Heraclitus has undoubtedly encouraged Char's philosophy to state that no matter how inherently noble truth is, the picture.we have of this truth is tragedy. But there is a relationship between the nobility of truth and the noble character of tragedy. This is the source of what we have been calling the antithesis, or the oxymoron, in Char's poetry. Man's ever-increasing awareness of his fate is equivalent to what Char calls the continuous presence of risk felt by the poet. This risk maintains the poet in a lofty position of attentiveness, of freedom of attitude and action. The risk represented by each poem is best understood by comparing it with the risk each day of living, with the threat involved in each decision of each hour in every man's life.

During the richest years of the surrealist movement in France, from 1930 to 1934, René Char was initiated into poetry and into a search for what the surrealists called *énigmes*. Char, who never disavowed his debt to surrealism, underwent many changes after that time. The quest of enigmas, for example, would not be applicable to his later discoveries. But there are images in his last writings that bear strong reminiscences of surrealism. A phrase in *A une sérénité crispée* (*To a Tense Serenity*) describes the dual character of man, which is repeatedly stressed in Char, but in a surrealist coupling of terms:

> *L'oiseau et l'arbre sont conjoints en nous. L'un va*
> *et vient, l'autre maugrée et pousse.*

(The bird and the tree are united in us. One comes and goes, the other grumbles and grows.)

A surrealist habit of looking at the world, of joining seemingly unrelated objects, has helped Char to express some of his deepest convictions about the nature of man and the universe.

As Char's writing became more and more visibly affected by the events of his time, he made a more conscious effort in his poetical work to transform what he saw and felt. But his art, seen in an image, is both transformation and interpretation. His poet's journal, *Feuillets d'Hypnos*, clearly states that he is opposed to the static, that if the alternative is the absurd, he will choose that because thereby he will move closer to the pathos of the world:

> *Si l'absurde est maître ici-bas, je choisis l'absurde,*
> *l'antistatique, celui qui me rapproche le plus des*
> *chances pathétiques.*

How lucidly the poet's vocation emerges from such a text! He is intransigent and refractory. His work is provocation and defiance. His system is unclassifiable because it contains all the opposites of our nature, all the dimensions of the absurd.

Despite the fact that René Char is a different poet in almost every sense, he has today reached an eminent degree of fame. The best way to approach him is by a study of those moments in his writings when he is aware of the poet's vocation. They are the moments of natural perception when he greets the world. This poet is essentially an analogist. The experience he relates in his books is not beyond the understanding of anyone who has intently and lovingly looked at the world.

Char initiates his readers first to his vigorous, sensuous life in nature. But from nature he moves quickly to the moral and the intellectual order. The final line of *Feuillets d'Hypnos* states the "ultimate reign of beauty" in the world: *Toute la place est pour la beauté.* There is really no poet in Char's system, there is only poetry. He is consciously bent on bringing back into poetry the strength of living men.

The vigor of this poet's mind puts him into a separate poetic world. We are moved by the vitality of his thought, but especially by the vitality of his concreteness. The truths of the world as he sees them are constantly demanding his allegiance. He is a poet characterized by the habit of seeing things charged with meaning— an ordered meaning regarding the relationships between nature and men.

In 1983 the Pléiade edition of the *Oeuvres Complètes* was published by Gallimard, thereby paying signal homage to René Char. He was seventy-six years old. For several years his admirers in France, Germany, and the United States had hoped the Nobel prize for literature would be given to him. As early as 1958, Albert Camus had called him "our greatest living poet." In this definitive edition, a long introduction by Jean Roudant is followed by 1,364 pages of text. Thanks to this admirable edition, it will be a simple matter henceforth to rediscover pages Char wrote over the years on Rimbaud and surrealism, on Hugo and Baudelaire, and on various painters. The poems of Char, composed over a span of fifty years, are now available in a single volume and testify to the achievements of a poet concerned with the gravest problems of our day and with the expression of these problems in verse.

Appendixes

I. Letter of Allen Tate Concerning Hart Crane and the French Poets

In early 1935, when I was studying Hart Crane, especially in relationship to Rimbaud, I wrote to Allen Tate in the hope of eliciting from him some clarification concerning Crane's knowledge of French. This very generous letter was his answer. I include it here with the conviction that future scholars will find it useful.

> 2374 Forrest Avenue
> Memphis, Tennessee
> January 26, 1935

My dear Mr. Fowlie:

I hope I shall be able to throw some light on your problem. As you probably know, Crane had little formal education. He had no systematic knowledge of English literature, and his knowledge of French was very limited. Rimbaud is difficult enough for people who know French thoroughly, and I am sure that Crane never read through any of Rimbaud's longer works. He was incapable of understanding any long work, in any language including his own, as a whole. He read passages, and from these passages he received some kind of stimulation that was often valuable to him; it often started a train of association that resulted in a good poem. About 1921 or 1922 he translated several short poems of Laforgue, and they are beautifully done—fine English poems and quite literal too, I believe, but for one or two slips. I haven't seen these translations for years; [Waldo] Frank either didn't know them or omitted them from the *Collected Poems*; I think they should have been included. If your library contains a file of *The Double Dealer* for 1922—I think the May issue—you will be able to examine the Laforgue translations yourself, and to see what a limited knowledge of French combined with instinctive insight into the original is capable of doing.

In general I should say that the actual influence of Rimbaud, or of any other foreign poet, was very slight. Crane had a romantic attachment to Rimbaud—he, too, felt that there was a similarity of attitude and sensibility. Perhaps it is a good thing that his ignorance kept him from really knowing Rimbaud; he might have been overwhelmed and stultified by the experience. Now that I think of it, although he had the complete works of Rimbaud about him, he used to read a book, I think it was Edgell Rickword, which contained some translations from Rimbaud by various hands. I know he studied this a great deal; he was particularly impressed by one of Sturge Moore's translations.

Of course he was immensely influenced by Eliot, in his youth, and by some phases of Pound; but by 1924 he was in revolt against these poets; and several years before he died he hated them in a definitely personal sense. He was singularly naive and personal in his literary judgements: Eliot to him represented "evil," or denial of life: so he dramatized himself, as the Affirmer, against Eliot. This, of course, was nonsense, and it pointed to a weakness in his talent; I mean the ill-repressed feeling of messiahship for American life.

Nevertheless I am sure that Crane's more than superficial likeness to Rimbaud is not without significance. The more I study this matter of influence, the more I am convinced that we must go carefully. It was not influence that accounts, in my opinion, for the parallel; I am convinced that Crane would have been essentially the same—except possibly for one poem, "Passage", which is interesting but not first-rate—had he never known anything about Rimbaud. I suppose the same thing was bound to happen to our romanticism that had happened two generations earlier in France. For this reason I think we may say that Crane's poetry came, historically, a little late, Eliot having already passed through that stage of romanticism before Crane had written a line. But this of course has nothing to do with the value of Crane—in spite of Pound, who is always worried about who did it first.

This answers your enquiry about as well as I know how to answer it at the moment. One more point does strike me here at the end. Crane knew more about Baudelaire than about Rimbaud. He was easier to decipher. He pored over the original, but he actually read again and again the Baudelaire translation in the Modern Library series.

If I can be of further help to you—as I hope I have been on this occasion—please let me know,

Sincerely yours,
Allen Tate

II. Letter of René Char on the Meaning of Various Words in His Poems

In late 1963 I was preparing for *Poetry* magazine (Chicago) a series of poems by four contemporary French poets. I wrote to each poet to request new poems that I might translate. René Char was gracious in his answer. He included in this letter several poems:

L'Isle-sur-Sorgue 2 sept. 63

Cher Wallace Fowlie,
Je vous remercie de votre pensée. J'y suis très sensible. Voici un groupe de poèmes pour votre projet. La moitié sont inédits, les autres viennent de paraître dans la revue "L'Arc," dans le numéro qui m'est consacré. C'est vraiment tout, dans la mesure du convenable, ce que je puis vous offrir. En tous cas, ces poèmes, à l'exception de "Chanson des étages" sont de 1963. Ils n'ont pas paru en volume encore.
Je conserve un souvenir heureux de notre rencontre à Paris, et vous prie de croire, cher Wallace Fowlie, à mes sentiments de fidèle estime.

René Char

P.S. Je suis à votre disposition pour toute question et éclaircissement concernant la traduction.

Dear Wallace Fowlie,
I thank you for your request and am pleased by it. Here is a group of poems for your project. Half of them are unpublished. The others have just appeared in the magazine *L'Arc*, in an issue devoted to my work. This is all I can offer conveniently. With the exception of "Chanson des étages" all of these poems are of 1963. They have not appeared in a book.
I have a happy memory of our meeting in Paris, and send you sincere regards.

René Char

P.S. I am quite willing to answer questions about the translation.

Encouraged by this last remark, I did ask Char several questions about his texts. I feel certain that my questions and the poet's answers will interest other translators and students of French poetry.

1. In the first poem, *Post-scriptum à Lettera Amorosa*, there is the phrase: je souffre d'entendre les fontaines de ta route se partager la pomme des orages. I asked for the meaning of *la pomme des orages*.

   Char: *La pomme des orages* est une expression très ancienne en usage en Provence, qui signifie le centre de l'orage, là où il est le plus dense et rond. On l'assimile au fruit (la pomme sans doute).

   (The apple of the storm is a very old expression in Provence signifying the center of the storm, where it is the most dense and round. It is doubtless assimilated to the fruit (the apple).

2. In the poem *Sept parcelles de Luberon*, the fourth line is "Doux fruits de la Brémonde." I did not recognize *la Brémonde*.

   Char: "La Brémonde" est le nom d'une propriété (maison de campagne) où mes parents me conduisaient lorsque j'étais enfant. Ce sont "les doux fruits de la Brémonde" que les vieux soleils ont fait mûrir, ces fruits tombent sur le sol, ils sont si nombreux que les enfants et les grillons mordent dans un fruit puis l'abandonnent pour un autre."

   (La Brémonde is the name of an estate [country house] where my parents took me when I was a child. The sweet fruits of La Brémonde are the fruits which old suns ripened. They fall on the ground and are so numerous that children and crickets bite into one fruit and then give it up for another.)

3. In the third stanza, *O Buoux, barque mal traitée*, I did not recognize *Buoux*.

   Char: Buoux est le nom propre d'un village dans une vallée du Luberon [a chain of the southern Alps]. (Quelques maisons seulement.) Une petite église romane en ruine et une tour—campanile qui est un vrai joyau. Buoux est comme une barque qui aurait fait naufrage quand les torrents du ciel pleuvent sur la montagne.

(Buoux is the proper name of a village in a valley of Luberon [just a few houses], a small romanesque church is in ruins, and a tower which is a real jewel. It is like a boat that was shipwrecked when torrents from the sky rained over the mountain.)

4. One of the poems is called *Chérir Thouzon*. I asked about the word *Thouzon*.

Char: Thouzon est un nom propre. C'est une colline, un monticule dans la plaine du Comtat (près du Thor, Vaucluse) où se trouvait au moyen âge une abbaye célèbre, aujourd' hui détruite. Le rétable de Thouzon est au Louvre, oeuvre d'un grand artiste du 13e siècle.

(Thouzon is a proper name. It is a hill, a hillock in the plain of Comtat [near Thor, Vaucluse] where there was in the Middle Ages a famous abbey, destroyed now. The altarpiece [reredos] of Thouzon is in the Louvre, the work of a great artist of the 13th century.)

5. I asked about the title of another poem: *Aux Portes d'Aerea*.

Char: Aerea était une ville de la Gaule Narbonnaise dont on ignore l'emplacement. Pline le jeune le signale entre Avignon et Orange. Je crois l'avoir retrouvée sur le coteau de Gordes.

(Aerea was a town of Narbonne when it was Gallic. Its site is unknown. Pliny the Younger claimed it was between Avignon and Orange. I believe I discovered it on the slope of Gordes [a town in Vaucluse].)

Selected Bibliography

French Editions of the Poets

The Pléiade edition (Paris: Gallimard) has complete works of eight of the poets I discuss: Char, Claudel, Baudelaire, Mallarmé, Nerval, Rimbaud, Valéry, and Verlaine.

Bilingual Editions

Baudelaire, *Les Fleurs du Mal*. Translated by Richard Howard. Boston: Godine, 1982.
Corbière, *Poètes d'aujourd'hui*. Paris: Seghers, 1951.
Laforgue, *Poésies Complètes*. Paris: Livre de Poche, 1970.
Rimbaud, *Complete Works, Selected Letters*. Translated by Wallace Fowlie. Chicago: University of Chicago Press, 1966.
Saint-John Perse, *Collected Poems*. Several translators. Princeton: Princeton University Press, 1983.

Critical Studies

René Char:

La Charité, Virginia. *The Poetics and Poetry of René Char*. Chapel Hill: University of North Carolina Press.
Mounin, Georges. *Avez-vous lu René Char?* Paris, 1946.

Paul Claudel:

Fowlie, Wallace. *Claudel*. London: Bowes and Bowes, 1957.
Fumet, Stanislas. *Claudel*. Paris: Gallimard, 1958.
Watson, Harold. *Claudel's Immortal Heroes*. New Brunswick, N.J.: Rutgers University Press, 1971.

Charles Baudelaire:

Bersani, Leo. *Baudelaire and Freud*. Berkeley: University of California Press, 1977.
Johnson, Barbara. *The Critical Difference*. Baltimore: Johns Hopkins University Press, 1980.

Kaplan, Edward. *Baudelaire's Modern Fables*. Athens: University of Georgia Press, 1989.
Pichois, Claude, and Ziegler, Jean. *Baudelaire, biographie*. Paris: Julliard, 1987.

Tristan Corbière:

Sonnenfeld, Albert. *L'oeuvre poétique de Tristan Corbière*. Princeton: Princeton University Press, 1960.

Jules Laforgue:

Ramsey, Warren, ed. *Jules Laforgue: Essays on a Poet's Life and Work*. Carbondale: Southern Illinois University Press, 1969.

Stéphane Mallarmé:

Cohn, Robert Greer. *Toward the Poems of Mallarmé*. Berkeley: University of California Press, 1980.
Fowlie, Wallace. *Mallarmé*. Chicago: University of Chicago Press, 1970.
Mondor, Henri. *Vie de Mallarmé*. Paris: Gallimard, 1941–42.

Gérard de Nerval:

Cellier, Leon. *Gérard de Nerval: L'Homme et l'oeuvre*. Paris: Hatier-Boivin, 1956.
Durry, Marie-Jeanne. *Gérard de Nerval et le mythe*. Paris: Flammarion, 1956.

Arthur Rimbaud:

Fowlie, Wallace. *Rimbaud: A Critical Study*. Chicago: University of Chicago Press, 1965.
———. *Rimbaud: Myth of Childhood*. London: Dobson, 1948.
Petitfils, Pierre. *Rimbaud*. Charlottesville: University Press of Virginia, 1987.

Saint-John Perse:

Honneur a Saint-John Perse. Paris: Gallimard, 1965.
Levillain, Henriette. *Le rituel poétique de Saint-John Perse*. Paris: Gallimard, 1977.

Paul Valéry:

Lawler, James R. *Lecture de Valéry*. Paris: Presses Universitaires de France, 1963.
Whiting, Charles. *Valéry jeune poète*. New Haven, Conn.: Yale University Press, 1960.

Paul Verlaine:

Adam, Antoine. *Verlaine: L'Homme et l'oeuvre*. Paris: Hatier-Boivin, 1953.
Bornecque, Jacques-Henry. *Lumières sur Les Fêtes Galantes*. Paris: Nizet, 1959.

Index